God's Love Offering: A Gift That Keeps On Giving

"Dr. Julia P. Marshall's Journey of Faith,
Demonstrating the Love of God & His Faithfulness
to Those Who Believe and Work Hard to Achieve"

By: Dr. Julia P. Marshall & Starsha M. Sewell, CSM, M.Ed.

DEDICATION

This book is dedicated to the descendants of the late Reverend Thomas C. Parker and the late Caldonia Fisher-Parker, who worked diligently with my father's brother Mack Parker and his children as well as the Mullen, Carradine, Peacock, Henderson, Harvey, Fisher, Stinson, King, and the Davis families to operate the family farm on Uncle Gus Henderson's plantation. Most of my relatives lived on the Henderson Plantation, attended Henderson High School, and worshiped at Mt. Herman AME Church.

God was faithful in providing for us consistently over the years and blessed our family with increase, and graced my father to serve more than fifty years in the Northeast Mississippi Conference as an iterant Elder supporting parishes and building churches in Grenada, Charleston, Oakland, Aberdeen, Senatobia, and Olive Branch, Mississippi. My father, Reverend Thomas C. Parker served as an Elder and received ham and other food items as compensation during our humble beginning.

CONTENTS

	Dedication	iii
1	Introduction	Pg. 1-9
2	The Beginning	Pg. 10-25
3	Happy Memories	Pg. 26-40
4	Birthday Collage	Pg. 41-49
5	The Marshalls Inc.	Pg. 50-60
6	Grenada & Beyond	Pg. 61-95
7	Lifetime Achievements	Pg. 96-132
8	Love One Another	Pg. 133-144
9	Livingstone College	Pg. 145-147
10	Journey of Travel	Pg. 148-177

ABOUT THE AUTHOR

Dr. Julia P. Marshall, D.H.L., is the former CEO of Marshall's Funeral Homes, Inc. She is a graduate of American University, Washington, DC, who also graduated *cum laude* from the American Academy McAllister Institute of Funeral Service, located in New York.

She is a selfless leader, who was honored with the naming of the dining area in Aggrey Student Union and the construction of the Julia P. Marshall Friendship Plaza at Livingstone College. Likewise, John Wesley AME Zion also honored Dr. Marshall with the naming of the Humanitarian Hall for her hard work, commitment, and dedication to her church family.

Dr. Marshall retired from a successful career in federal service, where she served for thirty-one years at reputable agencies. She dedicated her life to starting and growing personal, familial, and community-based business ventures that are proficient and productive because of the foundational wisdom that she invested.

She is a well-respected confidant and mentor to her strategic partners, who in her retirement are lifelong friends that keep her close because she is needed; and most importantly, she is always there. She is a compassionate visionary leader who broke many barriers without compromising her integrity.

Dr. Marshall has received many honors and awards for her outstanding lifetime achievements. Her impact is substantial. She is an inductee in the Washington, DC, Hall of Fame, the Livingstone College Alumni Hall of Fame, and the Democracy Hall of Fame, and she is an astute philanthropist and supporter of academic programs and scholarships.

ABOUT THE COAUTHOR

Starsha M. Sewell, CSM, M.Ed., is the CEO of an agile project-management training & professional development and faith-based intellectual property research firm "think tank" that provides customized solutions to complex problems in the areas of cybersecurity, business continuity, data analytics, and disaster recovery using customized research methodologies. Sewell's scholarly acumen derives from her professional track record in the field of higher education. She has served as a university professor, where she's taught courses in English, business, and economics.

Ms. Sewell is a professional member of the Authors Guild, the International Women's Writing Guild, and the Maryland Writers' Association, where she was elected to serve as Program Director for a chapter within the association.

She was the first African American Corporate Academic Dean at Strayer University, for its Global Region, in 2007 and is a subject-matter expert in higher education, graced with the ability to incorporate her scholastic, professional, and divine wisdom into products that aid in the faith-based life-skill development of individuals who desire more from the Spirit of the Living God.

Ms. Sewell is a faith-based motivational speaker, who is compassionate about women's empowerment and professional development. She is also a certified SCRUM master, servant leader, and an expert adult-learning, organizational-leadership, and training professional. Ms. Sewell is committed to using her God-ordained gifts and talents to advance the Kingdom of God, by creating and sustaining Kingdom-advancing businesses in the entrepreneurial space. Her motto is: "Integrity is the faith-based way to do business."

ACKNOWLEDGMENTS

Dear Parker family, I acknowledge and thank you for your support of my vision for **<u>God's Love Offering: A Gift That Keeps On Giving</u>**. I sincerely pray that you will be blessed in God's love, now and forever more.

– Dr. Julia P. Marshall

1. INTRODUCTION

It is with love and joy that I greet you today. I bring you greetings from the depths of my heart. I have been a blessed member of John Wesley African American Methodist Episcopal Zion Church for over seventy years, and I have served as a Sunday-schoolteacher, an usher, treasurer of the Church, trustee, and as a member of a host of organizations.

I will expound on my endeavors in other sections of this book, but I would like to start out by highlighting the significant role that servant leadership has played in my life. This work highlights my journey of faith, showing everyone who has labored with me in love and in service that with faith, all things are possible.

With this work, I seek to demonstrate the love of God, and I use examples of my lifelong achievements to prove Christ's faithfulness to those who believe and work hard to achieve. It is my prayer that you will be inspired to press past all challenges of life and break barriers designed to limit you.

The theme in this work is "faith," because all of my accomplishments were acquired simply because I believed I did not have to settle for common and acceptable professions to meet societal limitations at the time.

The ultimate takeaway from this book that I hope to impart is that you use your faith and encouragement to take a stand for your dreams and aspirations when others are encouraging you to sit.

African Americans paid a price for the freedom and liberation that we enjoy today. Our communities were built on hardships, struggles, and sacrifices; therefore, we must remain resiliently focused on the prize of freedom in the midst of barriers and opposition.

In this text, I want to relate some of my experiences as a Black American woman to others who can relate greatly to seeking freedom from all barriers, internal and external, that prohibit them from achieving their goals. With this, perhaps you will realize and be inspired to think that all things are indeed possible through Jesus Christ, with acts of faith.

I was born in a small southern town and grew up in a family of eleven children. My father was a Methodist minister and my mother was a schoolteacher and a strong supporter of my father's ministry. My parents reared eleven children: Clyde Cleophis, Clara Mae, Toscanelli, Naomi Pearl, Thomas Carey, Jr., Veola, Samuel Augusta, Julia Mae, Eula Lee, Mary Juanita, and Lafayette.

My father instilled in his children a strong sense of self-worth and would often say: "Despite the difficulties you will experience personally, your performance is what will ultimately count in your success in life."

My parents continually stressed the importance of having faith in God, and over time, I learned the importance of having faith in myself to believe in God making all things possible for me in my life's journey.

My life story provides evidence that God did so, just as my father said He would. I believed in myself and worked hard to achieve my goals and aspirations, and I was able to do so because my father believed in God on my behalf; so remember to pray for, and speak life over your children.

As I reflect on my parents' love for me, I can testify that God truly blessed me with the desires of my heart, but only because my parents first believed. I started out from humble beginnings, and for a short tenure, I was employed as a maid.

During my career transition, I was blessed with an opportunity to attend business college in Memphis, Tennessee, and after graduating from high school, I relocated to Washington, DC.

For a few months, I supported a family friend with babysitting services, before my career progressed and I landed a job in federal government as a clerk.

Over time, I was promoted to the role of secretary, and from there became an administrative assistant. With hopes of advancing my career in federal government, I decided to attend American University, part-time while working full-time in federal government; and with the power of God, I managed to be a good steward over the responsibilities that God entrusted me with.

I met and married my late-husband, Harold Marshall. Our union was blessed by God for forty-four years, and we accomplished many amazing things together. We started a chain of dry cleaners, and he supported my decision to continue my education.

My husband was an avid achiever, and his interest was in funeral services so we opened a funeral business.

I went back to school and graduated from the American Academy McAllister Institute of Funeral Service, *cum laude*, upon completing my degree at American University. We agreed that additional education would benefit our vision, and we supported one another in this endeavor.

It was not an easy journey, but we were committed to one another's goals and decided to succeed together. With hard work, faith, and sacrifice, we were graced with two locations for our business.

Our former business motto:

"One high standard and a belief that service is friendship in action."

WASHINGTON CATHEDRAL CHAPEL
4217 Ninth Street, N.W.
Washington, D.C. 20011
Phone: (202) 723-1250
Fax: (202) 829-1432

MARYLAND COLONIAL CHAPEL
4308 Suitland Road
Suitland, Maryland 20746
Phone: (301) 736-1616
Fax: (301) 736-1377

When I reflect on our joint efforts, and the goodness of Jesus, I truly believe that our marriage was God's will in action. We endured hardships, struggles, and many disappointments; however, with faith in God we survived and remained in operation from 1968 until my retirement in 2010.

In 1998, our funeral-home operation was subjected to a disastrous fire. This hardship was life changing because we had to rebuild our organization from scratch while battling health challenges. Mr. Marshall was afflicted in his health with diabetes and I was diagnosed with breast cancer. The breast cancer concealed itself for several years and was not detected until after I had surgery. The fire, diabetes, and cancer were several reasons for us to give up on our dream. These experiences were scary; I felt like my life was in complete disarray at a time when everything should have been working well.

After all, I was married, had a home, a business, and was pursuing the American dream; yet in the midst, disasters occurred. But with resilience, a strong support system, and my husband's prayers, I continued on my path to school and completed my degree. In all honesty, I wanted to give up, and even though I had successful surgery that removed the cancer, I still felt emotionally vulnerable because I was subjected to this health condition.

It was in these moments that I learned the fragility of life and learned the power of my late-husband's prayers, because together, we both pulled through and recovered the blessings of the abundant life that God had planned for us.

With lots of support from the community, we were able to sustain our business with a resilience that only God could give. God brought us through and He kept us together, and I pray that when you endure hard times you will think of this image and remember that with God's help, we made it and so can you.

If you are facing health challenges, remember it is okay to trust God and to operate in faith. It was only by faith that I was able to attend school, complete it, and recover from health challenges while also supporting my husband with his health challenges.

I know, firsthand, that actions form habits and that habits decide character and that character fixes your destiny. I encourage you to set your goals high, work hard to accomplish your goals, and when you reach your goals, be the best that you can be to maintain all that you have accomplished.

Upon, the death of my husband, in 2003, I continued to operate the business as CEO. I realized that our thoughts led to our purpose, and I watched our purpose go forth in action from habits that we established jointly while building together on our marital and professional partnership.

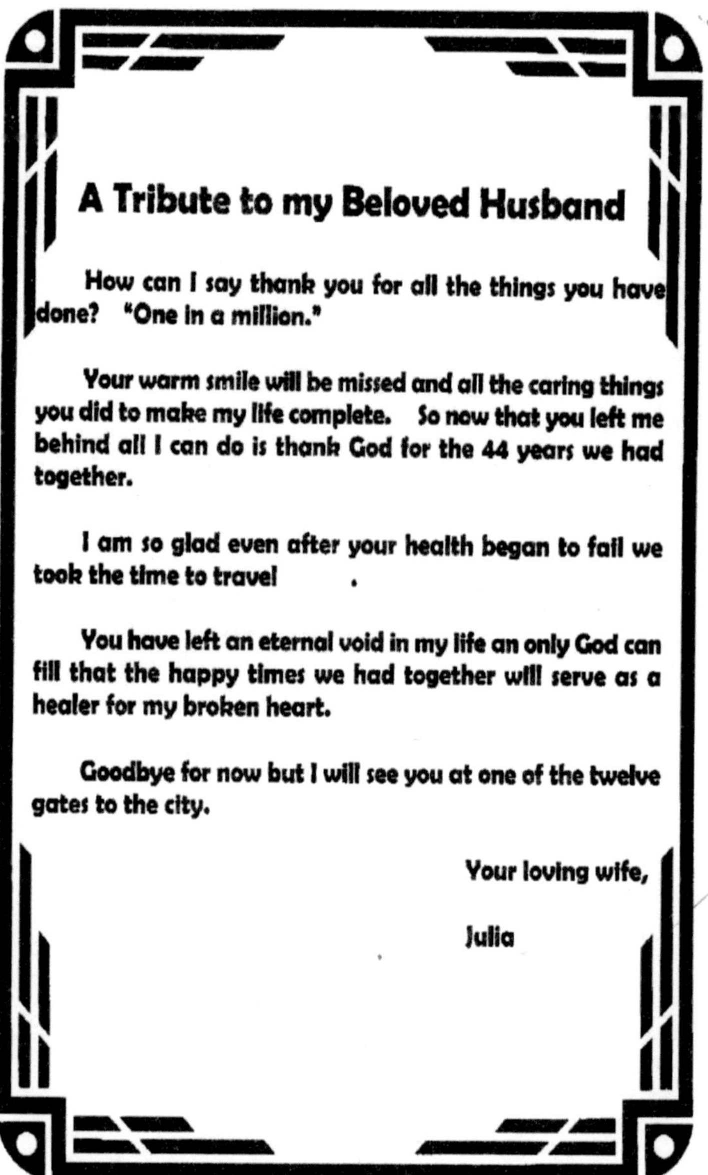

A Tribute to my Beloved Husband

How can I say thank you for all the things you have done? "One in a million."

Your warm smile will be missed and all the caring things you did to make my life complete. So now that you left me behind all I can do is thank God for the 44 years we had together.

I am so glad even after your health began to fail we took the time to travel .

You have left an eternal void in my life an only God can fill that the happy times we had together will serve as a healer for my broken heart.

Goodbye for now but I will see you at one of the twelve gates to the city.

Your loving wife,

Julia

2. THE BEGINNING

+ = Bishop Greene

I was born in Grenada, Mississippi and am the eighth of eleven children. My mother, Mrs. Caldonia Parker, was a schoolteacher and my father, Reverend Thomas C. Parker, was a Methodist minister.

Growing up, before, during, and after the civil rights movement, I learned the importance of remaining adaptable to the changing and evolving conditions of society. However, in spite of the negativity, I always believed that God had something better for me, and through my life's journey, I discovered that He did.

I was told that I was wasting my time by going to business college and that I would never get a job in business. Looking over my life, at this point it is safe to say that they were right—because I was destined to create, own, and operate businesses and was blessed by God to employ others.

Do not let anyone discourage you from pursuing your dreams; and never talk yourself out of your blessings. What God has for you is yours, so trust Him just as I did.

My family always had an entrepreneurial foundation as they were independent farmers. In fact, my Uncle Gus owned and operated a plantation where my father worked as a minister of the Gospel and where my mother worked as a schoolteacher.

My parents were proud of all of their children because we continued on the path of success from the foundation that they created. In fact, we created many small businesses that were meaningful to us, including seamstress boutiques, hair salons, and dry cleaners.

My late-brother Clyde Parker was a master tailor and a licensed demolitions contractor in the State of California; my late-sister Clara Mae Johnson owned a beauty shop; my late-sister Eula Lee Stokes made clothes and was a profound seamstress, to highlight a few.

However, I am deeply mindful that no one is self-made. We are all products influenced by our families, our church, other institutions, and people that have helped to shape our lives.

Our parents equipped us with tools of success, and we adhered to their instructions carefully because the Bible says so. Love and honor your parents and be obedient to the things of God, and you will live blessed.

Take heed of the instructions of your parents, even if you do not understand now; just be encouraged that God will take care of you because He blesses obedience.

My late-sisters Toscanelli Knox, Eula Lee Stokes, and Naomi Bonner owned the "Three Sisters Boutique." They were passionate about the fashion and hair-services industry, and they were professionals. I miss them dearly and am committed to keeping their honor with precious memories.

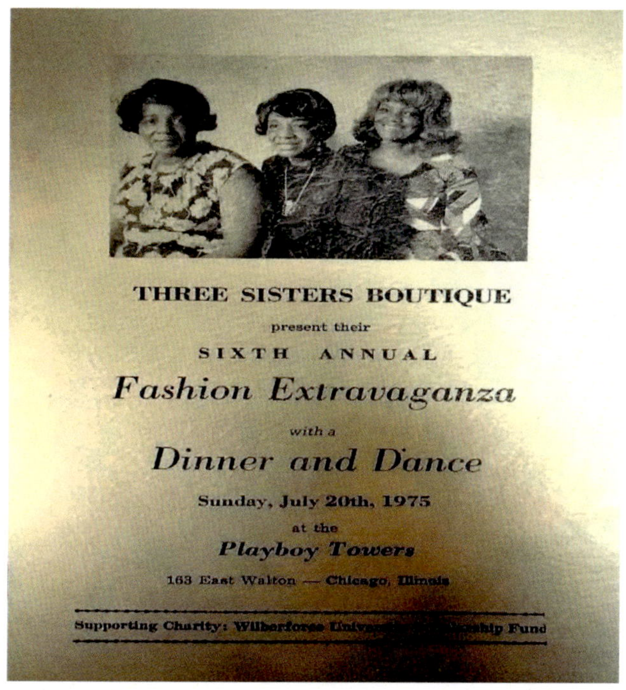

My late-brother Lafayette Parker was the best presser in dry-cleaning services and was employed by our business. He contributed greatly to the success and viability of our company and applied his talents and skills to help others. He never had a problem finding work because he was great at his craft.

My late-brother Thomas Parker was a soldier, who also owned and operated a dry cleaners while continuing a career in federal service at the United States Postal Service.

And me, Dr. Julia Parker-Marshall … Well, I am sharing the family legacy so that you can see the roots and heritage of the Parker family and the way our family is blessed because of my father's and mother's prayers, as well as the unity that we embraced in all of our endeavors.

My siblings (eight of my siblings and I are pictured below), we primarily worked for our independent businesses, providing dry-cleaning services, hair services, seamstress services, and home-improvement services to our local communities.

We also pursued and acquired real-estate endeavors with the family corporation and made great efforts to build and develop a future to last for generations to come.

Even now, our family still has a profound reputation for providing customized tailoring and seamstress services to clients. In the past, we held fashion shows for clients seeking authentic and unique attire, and to demonstrate their capabilities, the Three Sisters Boutique hosted memorable dinner dances and extravagant fashion shows.

The Three Sisters Boutique is still in operation, still owned by a family member, and I am extremely proud to see my sisters' boutique flourish in their honor.

Some of my siblings held careers in federal services but always remained faithful in assisting with the maintenance and operations required for our independent family-business ventures.

Always make time for your family, and please be sure to remember to pursue your passion along with your job. I understand that financial pressures sometimes take precedence over goals. However, when you create a plan to make your passions profitable, possibilities are endless and satisfaction is achieved. Faith the size of a mustard seed causes great things to be accomplished, so trust yourself to try and then work hard to keep your success.

I hold dear the memory of my siblings and I hosting the fiftieth wedding anniversary of our parents, Thomas and Caldonia Parker. Due to our careers and family obligations, we were not together as frequently as we would have liked to have been, but during this moment everything changed when my sister Naomi suggested that we gather together in family unity once a year following this anniversary.

Naomi's idea was so amazing that the family permanently adopted the tradition and continues to meet annually in diverse locations in the USA, in Toronto, Canada, and in Ocho Rios, Jamaica. Naomi and the family make our moments count by creating a plan; my advice to you is "make every moment count."

Never discount your perspectives but always honor your thoughts and ideas, because when you take small leaps of faith, it blesses you to move forward.

If you are standing still with doubt today, I hope that this illustration will challenge you to realign your thoughts so that you can take action toward pursuing your goals. If you are in a place in life where you have accomplished goals, then perhaps you should take that dream vacation, catch that plane rather than the bus; or simply just trust yourself to try something new, because it's never too late.

We are committed to carrying out the desires of our parents and my late sister Naomi and will continue to maintain the unity, love, and fellowship that they so amiably instilled in each of us through the example of family bonding and fellowship.

A family that prays together and pursues fellowship together is stronger together. I wanted to share this point of view with you because we all have natural gifts of leadership that can transform into transferrable skill sets from one industry to another.

Therefore, you should never underestimate the power of your ideas, because my sister Naomi's idea is still having an everlasting impact that blesses us continually. Always remember that humble beginnings are simply a beginning and that you have the power to decide the story that your life will speak. Operate in faith while trusting God for the expected end. Abundant lives are achievable, but you have to believe and work hard to achieve.

Then & now

Dr. Julia P. Marshall's Words of Encouragement

Ladies, I want to encourage you by letting you know that your voice in business leads to the development and maintenance of a democracy. Women today should be very proud of their rich heritage in the nation and must celebrate how far we have come, all while acknowledging that the best is yet to come. The role models, both past and present, have made their imprints an indelible impression through history based on hard work and dedication.

Women have been the compass and the catalyst to contribute much to our families, communities, universities, and churches. Our perseverance and faith have modeled and shaped other women, and our success symbolizes a beacon of hope of what is possible. I believe in leading by example and think that we, as women, have the willpower to strive for goals despite our obstacles.

If you look at the Bible, there is Mary, Ruth, Sarah, Deborah, and Hannah, who were all women of strength and of courage that endured varying faith challenges. Their stories tell of extraordinary valor as they walked with faith. If you look at women today, we've come a long way from women's suffrage, which gave us the freedom, the voice, and the power to be heard and seen, and it laid the foundation for women's right to vote.

We women have protested for the rights of our people and have challenged injustices in society as we followed our destiny; and I pray that you will discover and tap into your value today, because I am passing the torch and expect you to continue the journey.

Historical Women Who Broke Barriers

Historically, women have overcome great challenges. Here is a timeline showing barriers overcome by women who were willing to take a stand.

- 1833: Harriett Tubman started freeing the slaves.
- Pre-civil war in America, Sojourner Truth, a former slave and mother of thirteen children, rose up to become a preacher, orator, abolitionist, and a crusader for women's rights; in 1851, at a women's rights convention, she made the famous speech "Ain't I a Woman?" for those who wanted to exclude her because of her color.
- 1921: Bessie Coleman, known as "Queen Bee," left America and went to France to become the first African-American pilot.
- 1937: Amelia Earhart vanished while independently flying over the Pacific Ocean.
- 1944: Julia P. Marshall moved from Grenada Mississippi through Memphis, TN to Washington, DC to receive a Doctorate of Humane Letters from Livingstone College. She became the co-owner and CEO of a chain of dry-cleaning facilities and two of the most prestigious funeral businesses in the Washington metropolitan area.
- 1956: Rosa Parks started the Montgomery Bus Boycott.

- 1985: Mae Johnson was the first African-American astronaut to go into outer space.
- 1986: Oprah Winfrey began her first TV talk show, which ran for twenty-five years as she became a TV mogul.
- 2004: Condoleezza Rice became Secretary of State.
- 2004: Dr. Julia P. Marshall was conferred her Honorary Doctorate.

Today, we are blessed to witness the epitome of women's roles in politics. There are many examples of women doing amazing things in politics. Reflect on Nancy Pelosi, former Speaker of the House of Representatives; Hillary Clinton, who tried to break the glass ceiling with her candidacy for US President; and Sarah Palin, who ran for Vice President of the US. These women took action. What action are you prepared to take to achieve a goal or dream? The possibilities are endless.

I battled cancer while attending the American Academy, McAllister Institute of Funeral Service. Although I experienced moments of disappointment, I refused to become discouraged—I was determined to achieve my goal. If you were in my position, what would you have done? I decided to live, and with this life I accomplished my goals.

Someone reading this book might be in this position today. I want to encourage you to *live*. Live life even when you hear the worst news, because God has the power to change health conditions, circumstances, trials, tribulation, and people if it is His will. I am a living witness, because even with health challenges, my faith persisted and I graduated *cum laude*.

The picture above shows an important disparity in the funeral-services academic program. Women were clearly the minority in the male-dominated industry, but I was able to break barriers in the industry because I applied myself, and my friends did too. The women pictured with me below are also CEOs in the funeral-services industry, and we all attended the American Academy McAllister Institute of Funeral Service.

Thus, all things are possible when we work hard to achieve our goals. While I am retired, I still get excited about the barriers that my sisters are breaking in all industries, because we have so much to offer.

As you can see, through great sacrifice, women have earned the freedom to walk in unchartered territories and to compete for the highest office in the land.

Whether you are a Democrat or a Republican it was an exciting and electrifying campaign to watch women compete for national leadership opportunities. Dear African-American women, do you remember when Shirley Chisholm ran for President of the United States several years ago? With determination, and persistence we can do it: **YES WE CAN!**

As women, we all have a story to tell now that doors of opportunity have opened for us; we will not sit silently and allow racial and gender discrimination to stop us from fulfilling our God-ordained roles and dreams. Remember, it is by faith *and* work that all things are accomplished, as the Bible says: "Faith without works is dead."

3. HAPPY MEMORIES

Over the years, I have collected and gathered keepsakes that are near and dear to my heart. These items are significant to me because they serve as a pictorial time capsule of highlights of my experiences that I want you to enjoy.

BRIDE-ELECT — The Rev. and Mrs. Thomas Parker, Memphis, Tenn., announce the engagement of their daughter, Julia M., of Washington, D. C., to Harold Marshall. The wedding will take place in November at John Wesley AME Zion Church.

ICAN, DECEMBER 27, 1958 7

PRE-HOLIDAY WEDDING — Mr. and Mrs. Harold Marshall and their wedding party following the ceremony at John Wesley A.M.E. Zion Church. The bride is the former Julia Parker. Seated, left to right, are Miss Mary Frances Moore, Mrs. Arlene McFerrin, Miss Alfreda Raglan and Mrs. Helen Durham and standing are Oscar Sullivan, Charles Marshall, Mrs. Eula Stokes, the bride and groom, Robert L. Crouch and Clennie Murphy.

Secretary weds mortician in double ring ceremony

Miss Julia M. Parker and Harold Marshall were married Saturday evening in a double-ring ceremony at John Wesley AME Zion Church, 14th and Corcoran St., NW,

The Rev. E. Franklin Jackson, pastor, performed the ceremony before about 300 persons.

The bride designed and made her own gown as well as those of her attendants. She wore white chantilly lace, rose point pattern, over satin with seed pearls and rhinestones sparkling about the sabrina neckline of Empire bodice.

Her waist-length finger tip veil was attached to a seed pearl crown and she carried stephanotis, roses and orchids.

* * *

MRS. EULA L. STOKES, sister to the bride, was maid of honor. Her gown was a full-skirted rose net over matching silk taffeta, floor length, accessories to match.

Miss Arlene McFerrin, bridesmaid, wore torquoise blue silk taffeta, floor length, with matching accessories. Miss Helen Durham had on a bamboo gold taffeta and Miss Mary Frances Moore wore orange taffeta. All carried bouquets of roses.

Mrs. E. B. Henderson made the hats and gloves for the attendants, to correspond with their dresses and shoes.

The flower girl, niece of the bridegroom, was Cora Alfreda Raglan, Mr. Marshall was attended by Robert L. Crouch, his brother-in-law, as best man.

The bride's mother wore rose beige lace over matching satin and her corsage was pink carnations.

* * *

MRS. SADIE H. HAMILTON played the wedding music and Miss Naomi Cook sang "Because." Malcolm Taylor sang the "Lord's Prayer" as the couple knelt at the altar. The reception was held at the Kappa House immediately following the ceremony. Mrs. Frances Tyson, Newport, Tenn. oldest sister of the bridegroom, was honor attendant in the receiving line.

Mrs. Marshall, daughter of the Rev. and Mrs. Thomas Parker, Memphis, Tenn., is a secretary in the Department of State president of a local social club, teacher in the Sunday school at John Wesley AME Zion Church and vice president of the Spottswood AMOTT Club of the church. She was assisted in making arrangements by Mrs. More D. Tolbert and Miss Betty Holton, president and secretary of the club.

Mr. Marshall is the son of the late Mr. and Mrs. John R. Marshall of Newport, Tenn. He is a Pentagon employee and a local mortician.

Clennie H. Murphy Sr. was head usher and other ushers were Charles Marshall, brother of the bridegroom, Oscar T. Sullivan and Osie D. Hall.

Hostesses were Mesdames Marie V. Hewitt, Dorothy Mann, Louise Dennis and Misses Lucille Skinner, Edith Anderson and Annie Dudley.

The couple left for a brief honeymoon in Boston and New York. They will make their home in Washington, D.C.

* * *

OUT-OF-TOWN GUESTS included:

Sisters of the bride, Mesdames T. Williams, Juanita Cook and Daisy Acklin, Chicago, Ill.;

Mrs. Louis D. Johnson, Detroit, Mich.; Mrs. Oscar Parker, Chicago; Mrs. Naomi Pierce, Memphis, Tenn.; Miss Odessa Moore, Mrs. Myrtle Sumler, Mr. and Mrs. Ernest Wilson of New York City, the Rev. and Mrs. Thomas Parker, parents of the bride, Memphis, Tenn.;

Also, Mesdames Frances Tyson, Louise Raglan, Kate Allen and daughter Audren of Newport, Tenn., sisters of the bridegroom;

Miss Odessa E. Moore, Tarry Town, N.Y.; Miss Naomi S. Cooper, Miss Clara Snowden, Miss Neressa Innman, Mr. and Mrs. Alpha Marshall, Mr. and Mrs. Ernest Jones, Mrs. Mary M. Johnson, Mr. and Mrs. James F. Roseman, Mr. and Mrs. Clark Smith, Mr. and Mrs. LeRoy Johnson, Miss Helen Gipson;

Mr. and Mrs. David R. Mann, Miss Paula McLlain, Allavis C. Cousend, Mrs. Marie V. Hewett, Miss Inez Ramon, Miss Essie B. Davis, Mr. and Mrs. T. A. Brown, Mr. and Mrs. L. B. Barnes, Mrs. Bernice E. Williams, Mrs Clara M. Johnson, Mr. and Mrs. James Tolbert, Mrs. Daisy Acklin, Mrs. Naomi Pierce, Mr. and Mrs. Alfonso Moon, Mr. and Mrs. Clennie H. Murphy Sr., Mrs. Maggie Mitchell, Mrs. Sue McCollum;

Mrs. Dollie O. Litaker, Mrs. Rebecca Grimes, Mr. and Mrs. Samuel Blaxton, Leroy C. Morgan, Mrs. Dorothy I. Lewis, Mrs. Mary Midyette, Mrs. Beatrice L. Cookrell, Mrs. Eloise Bland, Miss Olivia C. Smith, Mrs. Beatrice Mack, Mr. and Mrs. O. D. Hall, Mr. and Mrs. Obediah Hannah, Mrs. Wanda Leona Brown, Miss Catherine Albitha Allen, Miss Elizabeth Gorman, Miss Helen E. Carey, Miss Beulah Carey, Dorsey C. Newman, Miss Grace V. LaSavage, Mrs. Alice Lee, Charlie M. Marshall;

Rev. and Mrs. C. D. Parker, Mrs. Tascanelli Williams, Mrs. Juanita Cooks, Mr. and Mrs. Herman B. Lancaster, Miss Bettie Holton, Mrs. Louise Cooper, Rev. and Mrs. E. Franklin Jackson, Miss Emma B. Evans, Calsar White, Miss Delores Johnson, Mr. and Mrs. Regionald Paris;

Miss Lucille Skinner, Miss Annie B. Clayton, Miss Odessa E. Moore, Admiral and Mrs. Walter S. Delaney, Mr. and Mrs. Harry G. Barlern and Mrs. Marion Ghelmini.

Memphian Weds In Washington, D. C.

Miss Julia M. Parker of Memphis and Harold Marshall were married Saturday evening in a double-ring ceremony at John Wesley A. M. E. Zion Church, in Washington, D. C., recently. The Rev. E. Franklin Jackson, pastor, performed the ceremony before about 300 friends and members of both families.

The bride designed and made her own gown as well as those of her attendants. She was most charming in white chantilly lace, rose [illegible] pattern, over satin with seed pearls and rhinestones sparkling about the sabrina neckline of empire bodice. Her waist-length tip veil was attached to a seed pearl crown and she carried a boquet of stephanotis, roses and orchids. The birde was given in marriage by her father.

Mrs. Eula L. Stokes, sister of the bride, was maid of honor. Her gown was a full skirted rose net over matching silk taffeta, floor length, accessories to match. Miss Arlene McFerrin, bride's maid, wore terquoise blue, silk taffeta, floor length, with matching accessories. Miss Helen Durham had on a bamboo gold, taffeta and Miss Mary Frances Moore were orange taffeta and all carried boquets of roses. Mrs. E. B. Henderson made the hats and gloves for the attendants, to correspond with their dresses and shoes.

The flower girl, niece of the groom, was Cora Alfreda Raglan. Mr Marshall was attened by Robert L. Crouch, his brother-in-law, as bestman.

The bride's mother wore rose beige lace over matching satin and her corsage was pink carnations.

Mrs. Sadie H. Hamilton played the wedding music and Miss Naomi Cook sang "Because." Malcolm Taylor sang the Lord's Prayer as the couple was kneeling at the altar. The reception was held at the Kappa House immediately following the ceremony. Mrs. Frances Tyson of Newport, Tenn., oldest sister of the groom, was honor attendant in the receiving line.

Mrs Marshall, daughter of Rev. and Mrs. Thomas Parker, of Memphis, Tenn., is a Secretary in the Department of State, president of a local social club, teacher in the Sunday School at John Wesley AME Zion Church and vice president of the Spottswood AMOTT Club of the church. She was assisted in making arrangements by Mrs. Moore D. Tolbert and Miss Betty Holton, president and secretary of the club.

Marshall is the the son of the late Mr and Mrs. John R. Marshall of Newport, Tennessee. He is a Pentagon employee and a local sport man.

Clennie H. Murphy, Sr. was head usher and other ushers were Charles Marshall, brother of the groom, Oscar T. Sullivan and Osie D. Hall.

Hostesses were Mesdames Marie V. Hewitt, Dorothy Mann, Louise Dennis and Misses Lucille Skinner, Edith Anderson and Annie Dudley.

The couple left for a brief honeymoon in Boston and New York. They will make their home in Washington, D. C.

Out-of-town guests included: sisters of the bride, Mesdames T. Williams, Juanita Cook and Daisy Acklin, Chicago, Illinois; Mrs. Louis D. Johnson, Detroit, Michigan. Mrs. Oscar Parker, Chicago. Mrs. Noami Pierce of Memphis, Tenn, Miss Odessa Moore, Mrs. Myrtle Sumler, Mr. and Mrs. Ernest Wilson of New York City. Rev. and Mrs. Thomas Parker, parents of the bride, Memphis, Tennessee.

Mesdames Frances Tyson, Louis Raglan, Kate Allen and daughter Audren of Newport Tennessee sisters of the groom. Miss Odessa E. Moore, Tarry Town, N. Y. Many others signed the register.

id-Winter

(Continued From Page One)

inery and abandonment of obsolete, wasteful plants. A normal 3 per cent advance in productivity would wipe out the need for 2 million workers in 1959, he said.

Secondly, the economy must provide jobs for about 1,250,000 of the present 3,800,000 unemployed to get back to a relatively low level of joblessness.

Third, about 790,000 newcomers who will join the labor force in 1959 must be absorbed.

"It is apparent that a restoration to the levels of production in the summer of 1957 (pre-recession) would leave us four million jobs short of reasonably minimum unemployment," Clague noted.

Christmas Holiday Starts December 20

Christmas vacation at LeMoyne College begins Dec. 20 and continues through Jan. 4, it was announced by the college administration this week.

Family Memories

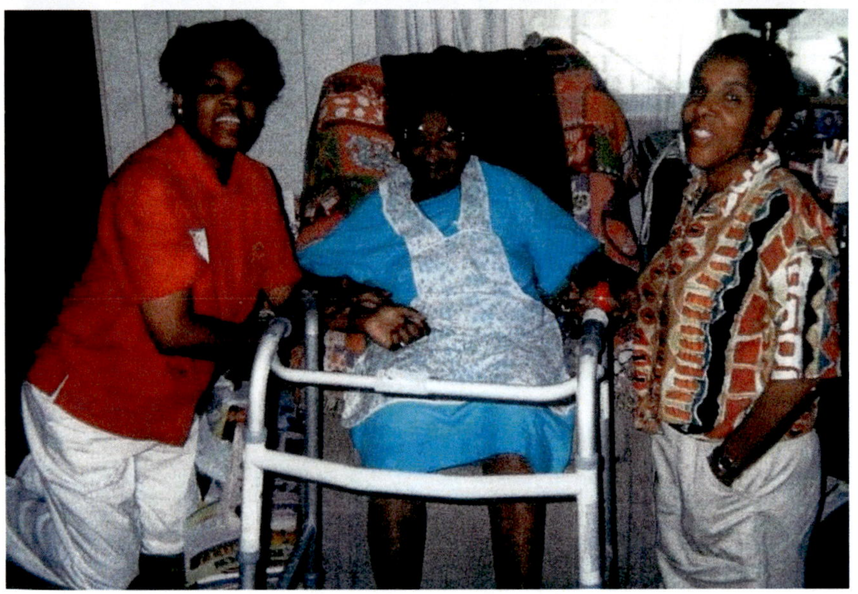

Memorable Times!!

Family & Friends

Enjoyable Moments!!

4. BIRTHDAY COLLAGE

HOLLYWOOD

HOLLYWOOD

MY FAVORITE BIRTHDAY CELEBRATION

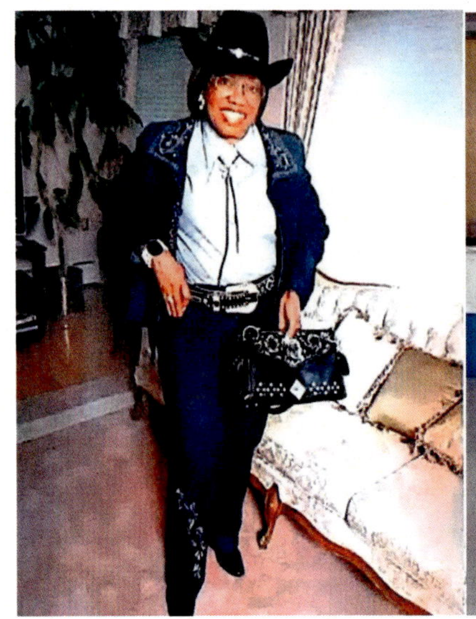

Dr. Robert L. Parker

5. THE MARSHALLS INC.

Our Company

Our Home

When I reflect on my humble beginnings, where I resided on a small farm in Mississippi, and then migrated to Washington, DC to become the CEO of two of the most prestigious funeral services in the Washington, DC area, when I look back over my life, I realize that I could not have imagined that God had so much in store for me.

In spite of it all, I always stayed in a posture of faith; and I am truly grateful and appreciative of my family, church family, friends, and supporters.

The Washington Sun • November 29, 2007 • Page 7

Dr. Julia P. Marshall
Business Woman/Ambassador for Christ

sephine Humble Kyles Woman of the Year

Born in Grenada, Mississippi, a small southern town near Memphis, Tennessee. She was the 7th of 11 children. Her mother was a schoolteacher and a strong supporter of her father, who was a Methodist minister. Her parents instilled in each child a strong sense of self pride and would often say, 'Despite the difficulties you may experience in life personally, remember, your performance is what will ultimately count in your success in life.' Her parents continuously stressed to them, 'If you have faith in God and in yourself, do you best at all times, God will make all things possible.'

Upon graduation from Henderson Business College, she was given the opportunity to move to Washington, D.C. where she got her first big Federal Government job (it was big to me). She started out as a clerk, typist and stenographer; then finally, she was promoted to Administrative Assistant. While working there, one day she asked for a promotion and was told by her supervisor, 'you should be glad you have a job in the government at all.' But her attitude urged her to

, she finally had to transfer to another agency. While working in the Pentagon, she met Harold Marshall
a very determined and confident man. He had an entrepreneurial spirit and when he quit that job, he
y worked together building up the business. He went out to pick up clothes and she worked at the clean-
ustomer service clerk. They developed the second largest black-owned dry cleaning chain in the met-
was working eight hours in the government, working nights at the dry cleaners doing alterations, and
that while they were running the drycleaners, her husband was also a

The Lord's grace and favor blessed me to acquire academic and business training, which was instrumental to my success. I cannot stress the importance of investing in professional development and acquiring a quality education. I am blessed to have served with my husband. We were ambassadors for Jesus Christ together, and I am continuing this journey of endurance for Jesus Christ.

I honestly believe that my achievements in higher academia equipped me with the tools that extended beyond the classroom setting; and when I think about how great God has been to me, I thank the Lord continuously for His grace, mercy, and favor.

As I reflect, I realize that God was preparing me with all the tools that I needed to give in my marriage, because I was created to be God's love offering to my husband. Our story illustrates the fulfillment of scripture, specifically Proverbs 18:22: "He who finds a wife finds a good thing, and obtains favor from the Lord." Ladies, I encourage you to walk in the way that God designed you to be. Proverbs 18:22 means that you were made to be a wife, and I want you to believe this.

Prior to becoming an entrepreneur, I worked in the US government for thirty-one years, holding various positions in the Adjutant General's Office, for the Department of the Army, Department of State, and the Agency for International Development.

I also worked as a seamstress because, despite my success, I never lost focus on my domestic skills. This was instrumental in allowing me to walk in the threshold of being a Proverbs 31 wife to Mr. Marshall.

Mr. Harold Marshall, my late husband, and I were able to see our dream manifest right before our eyes. With hard work and over thirty-seven years of faith in action, we established our first funeral home in Washington, D.C because I was prepared to give in marriage and fulfilled my role as God's "love offering" to him, which is a gift that keeps on giving. This is why I want to share my story and my late-husband's legacy with you.

Enjoy our photographic journey as I share business sentiments that were instrumental in the success of Marshall's Funeral Home, Inc.

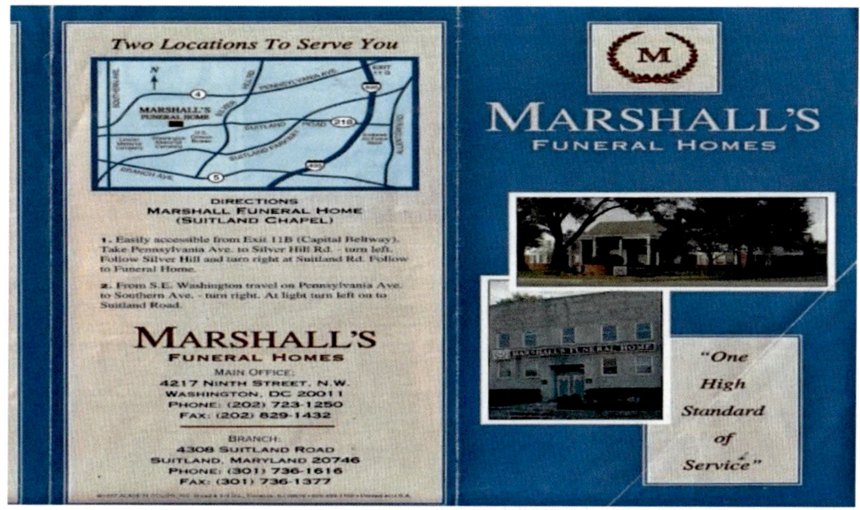

Funeral directing was perhaps an odd choice of profession for a woman, and, of course, the industry was male dominated. However, I was able to break barriers in the mortuary-science industry by developing and maintaining professional relationships and also by providing "one high standard of service" to all families, regardless of economic level, race, creed, or color.

It is my prayer that with the sharing of my story, my efforts will effectively assist the generations to come in achieving greater interest in faith, education, employment, marriage, entrepreneurship, business investment, community engagement, and community investment.

The group received varm greetings from Vice Mayor Sherman Lee durng the opening session n Monday morning. The elegation was honored to eceive words of welcome y Mayor David Bowers at Western Night" held at the ransportation Museum. he agenda included banuets, luncheons, seminars, endors, fun activities and uch much more.

The culminating event as held Tuesday night with esident Connie Steele, livering the presidenl address at the Awards nquet, reflecting on the eme "Honoring our Legy, Embracing Change to npower Our Future."

She expressed apprecian for being elected to a cond term and pledged to ntinue to move forward.

Connie B. Steele, President, VA Morticians Association, w award recipient Jack Miller.

The evening was filled with joy and excitement as Mrs. Rhonda Pleasants, funeral director and member of the Richmond Funeral Director's Association, was awarded VMA Mortician of the Year.

President Steele gave special thanks to the Western District Funeral Director's Association along with the entire VMA membersh for a great year. Spec recognition was also giv to her family, her Sororit Delta Sigma Theta, Th Links, The NAACP, an her Pilgrim Baptist Chur Family.

The Convention was great success and all de egated enjoyed being in th great City of Roanoke.

SENIOR MORTICIANS HONORED

Article credits and special thanks to the article producer (author unknown).

***

A Tribute to Ethel R. Poteat

"A life well lived. A race well run. And now she sleeps."

Ethel Poteat was no ordinary person. No one else was like her. She was SPECIAL. Her physical stature, personality traits, her habits, and her intelligence all made her one of a kind. She loved to wear her African attire, and she wore a hat at all times. She would also carry some kind of bag (a real "bag lady"). She was not the product of some cosmetic assembly line, she was unique.

Ethel was a cheerful, loving, and caring person who always brightened the lives of those around her. She showed great concern for others without regards for herself. She was committed to her family, her church, her friends, and her work.

Many times, when other staff members had gone home and there was still special work to be done, Ethel would stay right there with me to help get it done, no matter how long it took. She was a dear friend, and we shared each other's secrets and dreams. We were there for each other no matter what.

As my personal assistant at work, I could depend on her to keep me informed about both business and social events. Often times, she would serve in my stead. During the sixteen years she worked at Marshall's Funeral Home Inc., she endeared herself to many families, who loved her dearly. Her caring attitude captivated many families, and they would often request her to assist them during their time of bereavement.

Now that she is gone, a void has been left in my life. So too for our staff, who have always expressed their love and concern for her family. She was our notary as well as my personal assistant. But most importantly, she was my friend. Beyond our personal relationship, she was a valuable Christian, who loved God and lived Him in her daily walk. Her hands were outstretched to help those in need. She also loved to sing, not only with her church choirs but also in the community.

On April 30, 2006, under the auspices of the Business and Professional Women's Club, we were able to honor Ethel for her outstanding community-service work and to give her some flowers while she lived. Ethel's uniqueness will be missed.

I believe that she would have me leave this thought with you: "Don't be concerned about me now. I'm well with God. Forgive me for the wrongs I've done, and with the love that's left, thank God. Thank God for my soul's resting. Thank God for I've been blessed. Thank God for all who loved me. Praise God, who loved me best."

Reflecting on the loss of dear family and friends is never easy, but it is so essential to honor their legacies. As I conveyed, we gave Ethel her flowers while she was here, but I still miss her.

***

I am sharing God's love offering with you because it is my story and because it is a gift that will keep on giving: of hope, encouragement, and information about my heritage, because no matter how successful we are in life, we must never forget where we've come from.

My faith journey provides evidence that my Lord and Savior Jesus Christ has been so awesome and faithful to me. In fact, my tribute to my late-husband Harold, as well as my late-friend Ethel, conveys the void that I felt when losing them. But through this process, I have found there is healing in reflecting on the memories of all of my loved ones.

The powerful and mixed emotions that I experienced while reflecting on experiences have made me laugh and sometimes made me cry. However, through it all, the Lord has given me a newfound strength and a reason to rejoice. God has been faithful in healing my broken and contrite Spirit and is the restorer of my Soul.

6. GRENADA & BEYOND

At the beginning of this book, there is my family; and in the dedication section of this book, again there is my family. This is an essential reminder because you are so special to me. You are the reason that I worked so hard to achieve every accomplishment over the years.

My hard work and efforts and now my reflections are capturing past familial efforts to preserve the family heritage for the descendants of the late Reverend Thomas C. Parker and Caldonia Fisher-Parker so that you will always remember your foundation.

The Church: then & now

1838-2005

The new Greater Powell Chapel A. M. E. Church
368 Springhill Road
Grenada, MS 38901
Rev. Herbert Spears, Senior Pastor
Rev. James D. Holmes, Presiding Elder
Bishop C. Garnett Henning, Resident Bishop

Worship Services: 8:00 A.M. and 10:30 A.M.
Sunday Church School: 9:15 A.M.

Community Outreach:
Day Care Center
Greater Powell A. M. E. Church Senior Citizens' Homes

Mississippians Salute Dr. Julia Parker-Marshall

By Dr. J. C. Clark

Dr. Julia Parker-Marshall, humanitarian, churchwoman, businesswoman, civic leader and native of Grenada, Mississippi has deep roots in the Methodist tradition. Her late father, Rev. T. C. Parker, was an itinerant elder in the Northeast-West Mississippi Conference of the 8th Episcopal District (AME Church) for more than fifty years. He served and built several churches in Grenada, Olive Branch, Pleasant Hill, Horn Lake, Charleston, Oakland, Senatobia and several other congregations throughout North Mississippi.

Rev. Parker was the epitome of "Mississippi singing and preaching"; he had unusual exegetical abilities, started low, "tuned" up, got in "high" gear and ended up with a "whoop." Towards the end of his message, after he had exegeted his text, milked it for all it was worth in his search and understanding of spiritual truths, after he had submerged the awaiting congregation into the depths of spiritual profundity, after he had exhibited his skill and adroitness in hermeneutical and homiletical precision, and only after the selected pericope had been saturated with theological insight, holy boldness and "home-grown" wisdom that only a man with a "holy calling" could impart, he would turn around, "rare back", kick his legs up and holler, "Boys, I'm in some tall cotton now!" The congregation would go wild! Then he would ask them, "Do I know my lessons?" And the congregation would stand on their feet and shout, "YES!" Afterwards, he would turn to the Bishop and ask, "Bishop can I holler?" And before the Bishop could answer, the congregation would scream, "Preach, Pull-It, Go Ahead and Holler!"

As only a boy, I remember in 1965, when he preached the annual sermon during the Northeast Mississippi Conference (before the merger with the Northwest Conference) in Columbus, MS. The congregation was so enraptured and caught up in spiritual ecstasy that one of the women ran and jumped on his back, weeping, sobbing and shouting. Lay leaders of the conference including the late Dr. A. Charles Hunter, M. D. and the late Dr. L. L. Rayford, Sr., M. D. (whose son and grand-daughter are also medical doctors in Washington, D. C. and another son an Attorney in Baton Rouge, LA) cautioned him to "take his time", "hold his holts" with accents of "rich", "sweet", "glory", "ha, ha, ha", "watch him" and "fix it" by the other seventy or more ministers and the hundreds of congregants. The late Bro. Sam Knox, businessman and Pastor's Steward of Mt. Herman Church in Grenada, jumped up laughing, hollering and rubbing his hands together shouting, "He is a bad DELEGATE!" The forty or more Conference Stewardesses in their white dresses and black bonnets began walking the floor, shouting from pew to pew and praising God. (One even threw her pocketbook at Rev. Parker only to make sure that he had given it back to her after it fell on the floor; only then did she resume her shouting). The late Bishop W. F. Ball, Sr., of New Orleans, LA and Miami, FL, himself an outstanding preacher and "sweet singer of Israel", embraced him and wept. One of the venerable, sagacious, and spiritual fathers of the conference, the late Rev. T. J. Anderson, begged Bishop Ball to make him stop "before he spiritually slays all of us." However, Rev. Parker kept the spiritual fire burning and Rev. Herman Abrams, then of Aberdeen, now of McComb, jumped over the altar rail and ran out doors shouting. It took 5

to Dr. Julia Paker-Marshall by her late father.

This spirituality and Methodist heritage was nothing unique to the Parker family for the family that consisted of the Parkers, Mullens, Fishers, Carradine, Hendersons, Peacocks, and others had been AMEs for more than a century serving in the various twenty AME congregations in Grenada County, MS. (Dr. Louis Charles-Harvey, Ph.D., Th.D., former seminary president, immediate past Senior Pastor of Metropolitan AME Church in Washington, D. C. and presently Presiding Elder of the Potomac District as well as his sister, Wilma (former D. C. School Board member), are members of this family and have the same migration pattern from MS via Memphis to D. C.).

Julia was baptized in the Mt. Herman AME Church (founded in 1838 by the M. E. Church) in Grenada, MS at an early age. When the family relocated north to near-by Memphis, TN for better educational and economic opportunities for the large number of children, Julia and her family had the option of uniting with either one of the more than thirty AME churches in Memphis proper. However, they united with St. Andrew AME Church, one of the "flagship" churches of the city (Dr. F. D. Coleman, Medical Doctor and B. D. was the pastor) where the family was quite actively involved in the affairs of the church. However, her late father maintained his membership in the Northeast Mississippi Conference since the conference boundaries extended only a few miles from the Memphis city limits and several churches were located on the Tennessee/Mississippi state line. For a number of years, he served on the Conference's Board of Trustees, the Board of Examiners and on the Board of Trustees for Campbell College in Jackson, MS.

Julia migrated to Washington, D. C. from Memphis, TN and her Methodist upbringing dictated that she should join a "Methodist" Church. She united with John Wesley AME Zion Church and became actively involved in the affairs of her church. Mississippians and other AME Church members from the "deep South" often jokingly laugh that they had never heard of the AME Zion Church so when they move to the Northeast United States, they felt that they were "safe" within the "Methodist " fold so long as they see "AME" on the church's name, not really knowing the difference in the AME Church and AME Zion Church. However, Julia united with the church to worship God and serve in whatever capacity she was needed and not to serve nor worship denominations nor labels.

Julia has served as an active member of John Wesley AME Zion Church since the pastorate of the late Dr. E. Franklin Jackson. She has been diligent in her duties to the church while she actively worked in her funeral home business, making it one of the most renowned ones in the Washington, D. C. area. Aside from this, Dr. Julia Parker-Marshall never forgot to assist others in need and is always involved in humanitarian and educational causes. Her contributions to Livingstone College in Salisbury, North Carolina (the AME Zion Church's denominational) is only one of several causes she has supported as a testament of her love to the Church of God, young people seeking higher education and for unborn generations. "Many will rise up and called her blessed."

Mississippians throughout the state are very elated that this native humanitarian was born in our state and passed our way. On May 28 the Grenada City Council (where 4 of the 7 Black Councilmen are AMEs including the Mayor), the Mississippi State Senate (where 5 are AME Church members), the Mississippi State Legislature (where 9 are AMEs) and the Congressional Black Caucus (where 5 are AMEs including South Carolina Congressman James Clyburne) will declare this day as "Dr. Julia Parker-Marshall Day!"

As we embark upon a new year with Dr. Marshall in anticipating another great birthday celebration for next year, in remembrance of those who have crossed the bar and as a monument and testimony to our posterity, let's rededicate ourselves to the cause of right and righteousness and pray that God will send more sincere, dedicated, and un-selfish workers into His vineyard. "The fields are ripe unto the harvest but the laborers are few."

"Arise, Shine, Give God the Glory; for this is the Year of Jubilee!"

The 8th Episcopal District of the African Methodist Episcopal Church

3150 St. Bernard Avenue · New Orleans, LA 70119 · Phone (504) [illegible] · FAX (504) [illegible] · Email: [illegible]

Cornal G. Henning, Sr.

A Resolution

The Honorable Dr. Julia Parker-Marshall

Whereas, The Eighth Episcopal District of the African Methodist Episcopal Church, presided over by the Rt. Rev. Cornal Garnett Henning, Sr., recognizes the life and contributions of Doctor Julia Parker Marshall who has been an inspiration to thousands of people for a span of more than fifty years and,

Whereas, Dr. Julia Parker Marshall, a product of the Eighth Episcopal District of the African Methodist Episcopal Church, a native of Grenade, Mississippi and the daughter of the late Reverend T.C. Parker who served as pastor in the Northeast Mississippi as well as the Northeast- West Mississippi Conference and,

Whereas, Dr. Julia P. Marshall inherited from her parents the desire to serve God and her people through her knowledge, her work and her philanthropic spirit and,

Whereas, Dr. Julia P. Marshall's life work has taken her from Grenada, Mississippi to Memphis, Tennessee and finally to Washington, D.C. where she united with John Wesley African Methodist Episcopal Zion Church where she served faithfully since her affiliation and,

Whereas, Dr. Julia P. Marshall has distinguished herself in the business world where she is the owner of two funeral homes, one in Washington, D.C. and the other in Suitland, Maryland and,

Whereas, Dr. Marshall has been awarded the Outstanding Business Award of Washington, D.C., by the Business and Professional Women's Club, the Business Development Award by Delta Sigma Theta Sorority, Washington Chapter; honored as Soror of the Year by the Tau Gamma Delta Sorority, Mortician of the year Award from WYCB-AM Radio and inducted into the Washington, D.C "Hall of Fame" in April 20004 and,

Whereas, Dr. Marshall has distinguished herself as a philanthropist, business woman, a humanitarian, an African Methodist, a Mississippian and an American;

Be it therefore resolved that May 28th will be set aside in the Eighth Episcopal District of the African Methodist Episcopal Church as "Dr. Julia Parker Marshall Day." This day is to be celebrated throughout the Eighth Episcopal District and that a commemorative plaque be placed in the halls of Bonner Campbell Institute in Edwards, Mississippi so that all who pass through the hallowed halls of this institution will be reunited with this kindred spirit

Given Under My Hand and Seal this, the Twenty-eighth Day of May in the year Two Thousand and Five.

The Rt. Reverend C. Garnett Henning.

Presiding Prelate

The Rt. Rev. C. Garnett Henning, Sr., M. Div., D. D., Presiding Bishop

The City of Grenada, Mississippi

A Proclamation For The Honorable Dr. Julia Parker-Marshall

WHEREAS, Dr. Julia Parker-Marshall, was a Humanitarian, Businesswoman, Church and Civic Leader, Major Contributor to HBCU'S (Historically Black Colleges and Universities); and

WHEREAS, Dr. Julia Parker-Marshall, was born in Grenada, Mississippi on May 28, 1926; and

WHEREAS, Dr. Julia Parker-Marshall, grew up in the Mt. Herman A.M.E. Church in Grenada, Mississippi; and

WHEREAS, Dr. Julia Parker-Marshall, was inducted into the Washington, D.C. "Hall of Fame" in April, 2004; and

WHEREAS, Dr. Julia Parker-Marshall, won the Mortician of the Year Award from WYCB-AM Radio.

NOW, THEREFORE, BE IT RESOLVED by the Mayor and Councilpersons of the City of Grenada, Mississippi that we do hereby salute, The Honorable Dr. Julia Parker-Marshall, on her Seventy-ninth Birthday.

SO RESOLVED AND ADOPTED, this the 9 day of May, 2005.

CITY OF GRENADA, MISSISSIPPI

BY: Dianna Freelon-Foster
Dianna Freelon-Foster, Mayor

ATTEST:
Diane Spencer
Diane Spencer, City Clerk
City of Grenada

Presented By:
J. B. Flowers
Dr. J. B. Flowers, Jr., Phd
Councilman, Ward V

A
PROCLAMATION
BY THE SPEAKER OF THE HOUSE OF REPRESENTATIVES
AND REPRESENTATIVES ESTHER M. HARRISON AND WILLIE L. BAILEY
COMMENDING AND CONGRATULATING DR. JULIA P. MARSHALL
ON THE OCCASION OF HER 79TH BIRTHDAY

WHEREAS, on May 28, 2005, native Mississippian and Washington, D.C., resident, Dr. Julia Parker-Marshall will celebrate the grand occasion of her 79th anniversary of life; and

WHEREAS, a humanitarian, businesswoman, church and civic leader and major contributor to historically black colleges and universities (HBCUs) throughout the nation, Dr. Marshall hails from Grenada, Mississippi, born May 28, 1926, to the late Reverend and Mrs. T.C. Parker; and

WHEREAS, widow of the late Harold Marshall, Dr. Marshall is chief executive officer of Marshall's Funeral Homes of Washington, D.C., and Suitland, Maryland; and

WHEREAS, lauded for her unstinting dedication to educational support, community service and steadfast devotion to the A.M.E. Zion Church, while achieving remarkable success in the business arena, Dr. Marshall has been honored by Livingstone College with an honorary Doctor of Humane Letters degree, formal induction into Livingstone College Alumni Hall of Fame, the honorary naming of a dining facility at Livingstone College, induction into the Washington D.C. "Hall of Fame" in 2004, Outstanding Business Award of D.C., Development Award by Delta Sigma Theta Sorority, Soror of the Year by the Tau Gamma Delta Sorority and Mortician of the Year Award from WYCB-AM Radio; and

WHEREAS, as evidenced by her life of accomplishments, Dr. Marshall has been a vital asset to her community and is worthy of this honor on the commemoration of her 79th birthday:

NOW, THEREFORE, on behalf of the House of Representatives of the State of Mississippi, we do hereby commend and congratulate Dr. Julia P. Marshall on the occasion of her 79th anniversary of life and extend our heartiest wishes for love, good health and continued success in all her endeavors.

THIS, the 23rd day of May, 2005.

WILLIAM J. MCCOY, SPEAKER
HOUSE OF REPRESENTATIVES

ESTHER M. HARRISON, DISTRICT 41
HOUSE OF REPRESENTATIVES

WILLIE L. BAILEY, DISTRICT 49
HOUSE OF REPRESENTATIVES

PROCLAMATION

HONORING

DR. JULIA PARKER-MARSHALL

WHEREAS, Dr. Julia Parker-Marshall was born in Grenada, Mississippi, on May 28, 1926, to the late A.M.E. Church Pastor, Reverend and Mrs. T.C. Parker of Grenada, Mississippi; and

WHEREAS, she is the widow of the late Harold Marshall; and

WHEREAS, Dr. Marshall grew up in the Mt. Herman A.M.E. Church in Grenada, Mississippi and relocated to Memphis, Tennessee and united with St. Andrew's A.M.E. Church; and

WHEREAS, she moved to Washington, D.C. in the late 1940's and united with John Wesley A.M.E. Zion Church; and

WHEREAS, Dr. Marshall was inducted into the Washington, D.C. "Hall of Fame" in April, 2004; received the "Outstanding Business Award of D.C." by the Business and Professional Women's Club; received the "Business Development Award" from the Delta Sigma Theta Sorority (Washington, D.C. Chapter); she was named Soror of the Year by the Tau Gamma Delta Sorority; and

WHEREAS, Dr. Marshall received the "Mortician of the Year Award" from WYCB-AM Radio; and

WHEREAS, Dr. Marshall is a Humanitarian, Businesswoman, Church and Civic Leader, and major contributor to Historically Black Colleges and Universities (HBCUs).

BE IT THEREFORE RESOLVED, that I, BENNIE G. THOMPSON, MEMBER OF CONGRESS, am honored and privileged to present this proclamation honoring the long life and works of Dr. Julia Parker-Marshall on the occasion of her 79th birthday, on this, the 28th day of May, Two Thousand and Five.

Bennie G. Thompson
Member of Congress

Over the years, I have held on to my keepsakes in hopes of fulfilling this lifelong dream. I spent nearly eight years collecting and gathering information from each of you and want to express my gratitude for your love, support, and words of encouragement over the years.

As I reflect on your writings (pictured below), I want you to know that your hand- and typed-written works are so significant to the Parker heritage because your ancestors worked hard to achieve the skill set of writing.

I want to advise you of the historical barriers that the descendants of the late Reverend Thomas C. Parker were able to break simply by learning to read and write. My father worked hard and picked cotton after school, due to limited access to education, but he always communicated with his siblings and children with his written works. I have included below a picture of the letter that he wrote, documenting his frustration with being limited to a few days of classes and being required to pick cotton after school. My mother wanted the best for his children, and it is his determination that inspired my success. The letter is dated April 1967.

Rev. Thomas C. Parker

Memphis Tenn. 38114.
1851 Cley ave

Rev Thomas C. Parker

Mrs. Robert L. Parker Jr Roteiro.

do you know, you are A link in family record do beyound the civil war, my great grand parents came from africa to south carolina before the civil war, bought bought by a plantation white man name Robert William, he owned all the land in East 2, east of Grenada, mississippi, my great great Grand parents on my mother side was name bill davis, his wife name was name Isabella her mother was name grannie hanor, grannie husband was name, Kathenrick, this was my great grand

this was my mother grand parents, who was my great great grand parents, on my father side his father was name Starlen Parker, his wife was name henretter parker, my father had 4 brothers there were no out standing men among the long link family, untill my day, none of the families could read or write, none their children could read nor write until I came on the scene. I went to a public school one mont before christmas, a part of 2 month after,

but I made my way, the hard way, I went to what was called a subscription school 2 month in the summer, I started to reading a primer, I I finished it in 2 weeks, the next 2 weeks I finished a second reader, the last 4 weeks I was promoted to the 4th grade. I didnt have no one close by

1/ what so ever you know is right, make that your
standard, you have shown me the love you
have for me, the only one a long line of a
family that have come from the side of the Civil
war, you are the one grand son, other that can say with
assurance, that son- your grand father covered
his 4 score year, you & patricia is the only one I
have heard from thus far I want you & patricia
let this occasion be a higher day to remember, let
what you and keep a record in your memory the
gift you contributed on my 80th birth with good health
can read with out glasses. can walk without
A stick. you and patricia have given my flowers
while I can cherish them, this is one of the greatest you all
can do, this is telling me, you are not waiting till
I laid neath the clay I have sang many songs
but you too grand children have brought my dream
to pass, this first of this song I want you too remember
If you have any flowers, on my grave do bestow,
I would gladly receive them today, you should
scatter them now while I can cherish them so, do not
wait till I am laid neath the clay do not wait till I am
under the clay, let your kindness be given today
let your kindness be shown ne'er ere my spirit has
flowned do not wait till I am laid neath the clay) just
think these word over. This is the road I have traveled these
80 years. some times I wading muddy waters, some
times friend walk away. kinfolk failed me, but this is
my supreme age every year since I started out my promised

to help me, I was 12 years old in the 4th grade
with the other boys in my class going to school
every day and I was picking cotton every day
from sun up till sun down, sometime 4 miles from
home, when I reached 18th birth I saw I would not
get any where, so I would come home after sun
down, go to a Rich pine tree cut me an old bucket
of rich chips, go back home, eat supper, we only had
a tin lamp to read by. I put my bucket of pine chips
laid down with the light shining over my right
sholder, and read till got sleepy I was determ
ine to make it let me tell you something there is
no body in the world can make you fail, but
you, make it up in your own mind what you
wants to do, then go after it, there is too avenue
in life to pursue natural and spiritual, I advise
you, go after the spiritual first with in God and
your self. nine times out of ten, you will have what
you want. Some time I didn't see my children
from sunday. till sunday. for I would be gone
before they got up, and sleep when get back by
so doing I raised sixt girls & 8 boys, I will say for
them they did not have a bad reputation. I can pay
for them, they reasonable good children, and
all of you that walk like walked some day, some
happy day, when I come to the end of my journey.
you can tell the world that I was all smiles
when I met friend, as if to say I did find friend
to loose. I dont have time to find friend to loose

[illegible] now I have [illegible] [illegible] years or [illegible] year
[illegible] grace has brought me safe thus [illegible] grace will
[illegible] [illegible] [illegible] [illegible] [illegible] [illegible]
[illegible] I can't [illegible] [illegible] [illegible] [illegible]
and [illegible] I have [illegible] [illegible] grace brought me safe thus
far, and grace will lead me on. you [illegible] [illegible] tell what you can
do with you boy, Robert. let me tell you, [illegible] the [illegible] of
health [illegible] not pay. getting on the right road and [illegible], there [illegible]
because broad is the way that lead to destruction and [illegible]
there in because narrow is the path that lead to life and now and then
you [illegible] catch up with a, traveler the world of [illegible] [illegible] [illegible]
mean that it is narrow from the commands of God. we [illegible] a whole lot
just pretending. think on these things. you & Patricia [illegible] stay on the
right road, doing you know to be fair, because pay day is coming
and you dont want to reap what you did not sow, the world is
looking at you all, please excuse a little [illegible], I dont write often
so I just got to writing and could not stop to rest, so I am
praying both of you will have, a long and merry life, and continue
to hold high my record, that will be able to look back and see a well
spent life and before you a joyfull day; you both, [illegible] what
you too have done, tell her to join you. it is not what you say that counts
but what you do, tell her its not what she [illegible] to do, [illegible] but what she
has done, that counts, dont wait, till I die, to bring roses, but bring
them while I can cherish them, hoping for you all a long successfull life
I will be ever your grand father,

Rev. Thomas C. Parker,

2017 Parker Family 56th Reunion. How appropriate to share these words of thankfulness for the "seventh" wonder of our grandparents, the Rev. Thomas C. Parker and Caldonia Fisher Parker

Dr. Julia P. Marshall, matriarch, philanthropist, scholar, businesswoman fashion extraordinaire and most importantly, child of God, words cannot express the appreciation of love, caring, support, and giving you have provided for me and my family throughout the years. So as I take this moment to share these thoughts for you to peruse later I say with heart felt thanks and appreciation thank you, thank you, thank you for being my aunt, mother mentor, confidant and friend throughout my life.

May you continue to enjoy the blessings of God and the fruits of your labor until He says, well done thou good and faithful servant take thy rest.

With love and gratitude,
your niece,

Patricia Upton

Humbly submitted
Sunday, July 23, 2017

The years seem to have flown by. As I have watched our family Dwindle down, to where we are today out of Eleven loving Aunts & Uncles We are down to one who is the Matriarch of the Parker family Julia P Parker' has been Blessed because of her Goodness, God has

Bless her beyond her own Imagination And she has Gladly & Selfishly Shared With her Family her Blessing May God Continue to bless & Keep her

Hallmark

Charles Pepper

MADE WITH PAPER FROM WELL-MANAGED FORESTS
MADE IN CHINA

7-23-17

Dearest Aunt Julia ~

We are honored being related to you. Your hardwork and dedication to your faith, family and work serves as a shining example for all to follow. Through all of your success in life, you remain humble and blessed. Loving You Victor, Angela, Kimora

Dear Aunt Julia,

Life with you is Lovely. I have witnessed you being a blessing to so many People in the family including my household, and I would like to say thank you for every thing you have done for my family and I. I Love you Aunty

Sincerely [signature]

Dear Aunt Julia,

You have been very supportive of my academic life. You have given me inspiration and encouragement when I needed it most; and most importantly, you have taught me the meaning of dependability. I wouldn't have made it through my first year of college financially if it wasn't for you. So thank you.

Sincerely,

Joseph Upton Jr

-Ps, Thank you for your prayers as I am recovering.

To Lead a family
Comes great responsibility.
The help you give
Roots from your unconditional
Love. The Leadership,
scholarship
wisdom you and and
to mold us holds helps
us a Rolemodel and give
that we are Lucky
and greatful to call
our family and
for that we say thank you.

Auntie Julia:
Derrick + Wendy Parker Would
Like to Say "Thank you for
All of you Love, your Support
you are our back bone" And
we Say (Thank you) we Luv U

7-23-17
Praise God for Aunt Julia, for
being THE EVIDENCE, that reaching
for the sky is NOT just DOABLE!!
But WE, mere blacks, can achieve
ANYTHING! So many times over the
many years I've had the opportunity
to share my Aunts: INGENUITY and
ENTREPRENEURSHIP, her PIZZAZ and
of course her STYLE, with doubters
+ NONBELIEVERS. I Love you
Autie, Lolita

Dear Aunt Julia,

I want to thank you for being a strong support system for the family when one part of the family falls you'll always, whether its emotionally or finacially step in and help out where you can without even being asked. When my brother had his incident all the way in atlanta, you helped make a way for my parents to get to him. This has taught me that when I need family they are one call away and to be able to do the same when the time comes.

7/15/17

To my other mama,

You are an AMAZING woman. I admire your strength, courage, compassion, style, and sassiness. I don't know what I did to deserve you but I am blessed that God saw fit to bless me with you not only as my aunt but as my godmother.

I appreciate everything you have ever done for me. I know we don't get many of them but I cherish the moments we do get to share together; the make-up classes, the late night piddling, and our face time conversations. I know sometimes it seems as if the world is on your shoulders, people always got their hand stuck out, and you feel taken advantage of, unappreciated and used. I see you hurt when people make promises and don't keep them but that never stops you from giving. You are the true epitome of a woman, and the real definition of a QUEEN.

I must say having two mothers ain't always easy because when I'm wrong or make bad decisions, I get "it" from both ends, but I would not change it for the world. I am truly blessed.

Thank you for being YOU.

Love forever and always,

Your goddaughter,

Tyke

Thank you for everything! You are greatly appreciated for all that you do. We love you!

-Kiana ♡

Aunt Julia,

We are so blessed to have you as our matriarch.

Love you!

Ivy Pierce

Faith, hope, and love.
all three represent you aunt Julia!
But the greatest of these is love.
God bless and keep you always.

-Love Renee

Aunt Julia you have been a inspiration in my life I thank you and love you for that. Love you

Sam

Congratulations Aunt Julia on your outstanding recognition from the One Hundred Black Women Organization You have been a lightening rod which is demonstrated by your success. Your life reads like a good book which reveals the content of your character, your entreprenuerialship, your spirit as a philanthropist and community activist have been outstanding. There are so many chapters that capture the blueprint for your success. The family thanks you for the rich legacy and the roots you've established for all the generations to witness. We are so proud of you and all your accomplishments. We hope you keep accelerating because, we're waiting to read the next chapter of the dynasty you built through dedication and perseverance. You took the road less traveled and God has blessed you for not only who you are but for being the champion and embracing causes that has enriched the lives of others.

Your generosity of giving and your quiet demeanor accentuates your beauty as the Queen of our family. You truly are a woman of strong conviction, commitment and courage. You are as electrifying, as you are beautiful. We thank the One Hundred Black Women for acknowledging you because There is no greater honor than being recognized by not only your own kind but by your own gender.

We hope God continue to Bless and Keep.

Love,
The Parker Family
From
Coast to Coast

July 18, 2017

Aunt Julia,

Sorry we couldn't make it. Thanks for letting us stay at your house. I hope we will be able to come back. Miss you.

Your nephew,

Kadyn

Kadyn Harper

Dear Aunt Julia:

When the phrase "Phenomenal Woman" is mentioned you, Aunt Julia, immediately come to mind.

You are a living inspiration and reminder of what a person can become and do when one trusts in God and moves forward in faith, with determination, perseverance and courage.

Your unconditional love and devotion and generosity to all of us who are blessed to have you in the family is most touching. The things you have accomplished are truly amazing and inspirational as witnessed by the numerous awards and commendations publicly given to you. Your contributions to your community -whether through your church, your sorority, the charities you support and of equal importance of yourself and your time exemplifies the true spirit of giving. I thoroughly appreciate and am grateful for the gift of knowing you are my aunt.

Finally, the dignity and grace with which you carry yourself that contribute to the beauty of your spirit, these things are parts of the reason why when "Phenomenal Woman" is mentioned, you immediately come to mind.

Aunt Julia, you are greatly admired, very much appreciated, and you are deeply loved.

With the utmost respect and regards, and sincere good wishes for your continued well being

Your niece,

Doris

July 18, 2017

Dear Aunt Julia,

How is everything going? Are you still moving like a kid? You might be 92 but you move around like your 20. Anyways I just wanted to check in and see how you are doing. Sorry I couldn't make it to the family reunion so I sent a letter in my presence. Hope you have more pleasant memories!

Your little buddy,

Trenton H.

July 18, 2017

Aunt Julia,

Let me first say the words that are in our hearts but were not always spoken (I LOVE YOU). In the last few years I have grown to know who you are. You make me feel proud to have Parker blood running through my veins. You make me want to be a better person you're; a Godly woman, kind, loving, caring, smart, quick-witted, just to name a few but let's not leave out, sensitive, most people don't know how sensitive you are and that you do hurt when promises aren't taken seriously. I love you thank you for allowing me and trusting me to come into your home and do what I do. (NOT PAPER WORK) I enjoy checking on you even though at times I feel that every day may be a bit much at times, I don't want you to get sick of me. I plan to see you again before the year is out, have the list ready.

Love You,

Claudette

Claudette

Tuesday, July 18, 2017

Dear Aunt Julia,

I have seen your Hawaiian picture from your 92nd birthday party. It looked like you are 40 years old. At first I didn't know who it was on the picture, until Granny told me. You look so beautiful, I am so glad you're my great aunt. Sorry we couldn't make it to the family reunion, so hope you enjoy my letter. I wish I was there so I could give you a big hug.

Your Great Nephew,

Jordyn

Jordyn Watson ☺

Aunt Julia, we were taught us that if you could dream, you could reach for the stars.
However, you demonstrated that in life you can put your imprint on the moon through your hard work and dedication.

You are the ICON of this family because you took the road less traveled. We can only surmise that there were many challenges that you faced, but your valor,
determination and intellect became a bridge which led to the gateway and hallmark
of your success and empire.

We thank you for a job well done and being the role model of this family so take
your well deserved rest for you surely surpassed all the tests.

Your generosity as a philanthropist have touched so many lives and opened many
doors for others to EXCELL. WHAT A TESTIMONY!!!!!

There is an old adage that says to much that is given much is expected. Your 60
years of dedication have placed you in an elite league of your own which made you
the star of this family, and we hope you continue to shine so bright.

We crowned you as Queen of this family when you became an octogenarian and now we give you your slippers so take your rest. Plan many trips as you embark on retirement
after 6 decades of hard work and determination. What a Milestone, what a Journey,
What a Life so forge ahead as you've passed the reign.

We hope God continue to bless you with longevity and good health all the days of your life.

Much Love,

James and Olivia Parker

It was not uncommon for my father to write letters to me, but the letter that I hold dear to my heart is the item pictured below, where "Papa" stated:

Mrs. Julia P. Marshall, Dear Daughter this come to let you know that I received your loving letter so you will know we are all doing fine.

"I have planted my garden and it is growing off fine. I have set out 4 rows of onions, 1 row of tomatoes, 2 rows of sweet potatoes, 2 rows of corn, 1 row of cucumbers, and 1 row of bunch beans.

I keep busy every day. The gals began to call me every week. I tell the children Laf, Needa, Marva, TC and Mary, if the reunion don't have the money I can give all that I have. I am too old now to try to make love with any woman now, don't worry about me, Caldonia carried all the love I had with her. She did not leave me with enough to worry about, if I can live these 20 years in peace so when I go where she is, I can look behind me and relive a well spent life as we did before.

It will be a joyful day, when I can hear Him saying to me. Whom I am serving come on up higher, you have been faithful over a few things and enjoy the blessings I have prepared for you; that's about all. My highest ambition is just don't make no mistake thinking you are serving Him at the same time that you are looking back at the things of this world.

Put not your trust in riches, and lose your soul; what profit a man has when he gain the world and loose his soul, think on these things try to live a righteous life, it will pay off on pay day. For pay day is coming, look back at the long way I have come.

First think, what troubles I have seen; what conflicts I have passed; but out of it all the Lord has brought by His love, and still he does. His help afford and hides our lives above. Your loving Father, Rev. T.C. Parker

4. 27. 70

Memphis Tenn

Mrs Julia P. Marshal

324 Oneida st Washington D. C.

Dear Daughter, this Come to let you know that have received your loving letter so you will know we are all doing fine. I have planted my garden and it is growing fine. I have planted and set out 4 rows of onion, 1 row of tomatoes 2 rows of sweet potatoes, 2 row of corn 1 row of ish potatoes 1 row of Cucumbers 1 row of bunch beans, I keeps busy every day, the gals began to calling me every week, I tell the children, Loyf, Needa, Marza TC, and Mary, if the women got some money I can get that about all they have I am interested in or I can use, I am too old now to try to make love with any woman now, dont worry about me, Caldonia carried all the love I had with her. she did not leave me enough to worry about. if I can live these 20. years, I willing to leave all the love I have left to you 9. children. you all just help me live these 20. years in peace, so when I go where she is, I can look behind me and see like her, a well spent life and before

me a joyful day, when I can ~~hear~~
hear him saying to me, whom I am
serving Come on up higher, you have
been faithful over a few things and
enjoy the blessing I have prepared for
you thats about all, my highest
ambiskion, just dont make no
mistake, thinking you are serving
him, at the same time you are
looking back at the thing of the world
Put not your trust in riches, and
loose your soul, what profit a man
has when he gain the world and
loose his soul, think on these things
try to live a righteous life it will
Pay off, Pay day, for Pay day is coming
look back at the long way I have come
just think what troubles have I seen,
what conflicks have I passed, but out of
all, the lord, has brought by his love.
and still he does his help afford and
hides our lives above, your loving
father Rev T C, Parker

♥

♥

♥

Let's focus on "God's love offering," the journey of community support, engagement, and reinvestment, because our roadmap to success was not an easy journey. We were committed to treating and caring for families with love, dignity, and respect, and we always wanted them to know that we were available not only during the difficult times but also during better days.

Marshall's Funeral Home, Inc. spent long hours serving the community by conducting seminars, supporting church programs, and funding scholarship programs, and we also created summer employment programs.

We took risks, with faith, and reinvested in our business to ensure its sustainability and viability. We struggled because doing business was not always glitz and glamour, but with perseverance, determination, wise budgeting, and a vision, we managed to build a reputable organization that was well respected and appreciated by our community.

March 22, 1984

Dear Mrs. Marshall:

We are writing this letter in appreciation for all services rendered in regard to the funeral of our deceased uncle Rev. George W. Thomas on March 20, 1984. We would like to sincerely thank you for showing such great concern in our hour of need.

We could never express the gratitude we feel in regard to your referring us to apply for burial assistance at the DHR. We had visited several funeral homes, but not one mentioned that the service was available; even after we explained our plight. We will never forget you for this act of kindness.

The assistance offered by the driver in attendance at the family home at [illegible], was beyond reproach. He was sympathetic, patient, very understanding and helpful; even offering assistance after arrival at the funeral home.

The beautiful, young lady in attendance during the service was very thoughful, extremely kind and concerned in assisting the family members; always ever present to assure them she was there if needed.

Also, we were very impressed with the officiating minister (Rev. George Davis), his words of inspiration were very comforting to the family and did not induce a lot of undue suffering.

We know that the above mentioned things may be a daily routine for you and your staff, but we feel that you all should be commended for giving so very much of yourselves in our time of bereavement.

In summary, we have never attended a funeral that we could describe as joyous, but this one was very close to it. The entire family loved my uncle very much, and we would like to thank you and your wonderful staff for rendering such a beautiful work of art on the body and the funeral.

Sincerely,

Mrs. Gloria D. McNair and
Mrs. Margie R. Fowler

Let's sidebar for a minute. I would like to share my resume with you that I used when I was actively working. I challenge you to update your resume and to create that business plan that is your heart's desire. I redacted confidential information, and although this resume has aged substantially, I hope that it will inspire you. **You Can Do It!**

Resume of Dr. Julia P. Marshall

Dr. Julia P. Marshall

EXECUTIVE MANAGEMENT

Entrepreneurship & Expansion • Strategic Planning • Death care • Humanity/Philanthropy

Highly accomplished visionary Executive Officer with extensive hands-on experience in ownership, management and business leadership, and strategic planning with both startup and growth operations of multi-million dollar funeral service enterprises. Chief Executive Officer / Secretary-Treasurer with an established record of success in significantly working with various boards, churches, banks, associations, attorneys, and local governments, solving business issues while managing costs and risks, and growing enterprise value from serving four families per month to over 900 families per year. Results-oriented decisive leader and team player, strong in cash forecasts, directing major projects, problem solving, strategic positioning, and profitability. Tendency to thrive in dynamic and fluid environments while remaining focused and pragmatic. Areas of expertise in:

- Visionary Leadership
- Operations Management
- Financial & Strategic Planning
- Insurance Agent & Notary Public
- Staff Management, Training & Development
- Funeral Services
- Humanities
- Accomplished Spokesperson

Over 32 years of expertise in supporting funeral service business through critical start-up, or turnaround situations, and coordinating rapid-growth market expansions. Responsible for managing all personnel activities which include recruiting, hiring, reclassification/promotions and salary management. Ensured compliance with governmental regulations and established industry standards. Responsible for securing several government contacts and initiating and developing in-house training. Proven ability to work independently as well as a team member. Exercise a high degree of discretion, mature judgment, and tact in handing issues of a sensitive nature.

PROFESSIONAL EXPERIENCE

MARSHALL'S FUNERAL HOME, INC. – Washington, DC 10/68-[redacted]
MARSHALL'S FUNERAL HOME OF MARYLAND, INC. – Suitland, MD 07/92-[redacted]

Chief Executive Officer / Secretary-Treasurer

Serves as CEO / Secretary-Treasurer of multi-million dollar two locations funeral service business [redacted]

Direct all operations of business. Full responsibility for bottom-line factors, including company vision, long-range strategic planning, and management. Serves as Secretary-Treasurer since the inception of the company in October of 1968. Redefine organizational structure, oversee major pricing decisions, and perform monthly financial evaluation of business results. Provides cross-functional management; directs three managers (DC, MD, Preneed), and general oversight of 35 employees. Enhanced company stature and stimulated sales through the design, development and adoption of profitable business opportunities. Negotiated, prepared and executed [redacted] renovation / remodel construction project for the business.

Key Achievements:

- Successfully identified and resolved problems as team-player resulting in promotions within the office
- Recipient of Thirty-One (31) Years of Outstanding and Dedicated Service Award from the U.S. Government, on June 30, 1975
- Analyzed and researched the viability of complex proposals, resources necessary for entering negotiations within diplomatic arena
- Provided specialized advice in international culture negotiations
- Recommended program resources and prepared documents for high ranking government officials
- Assisted in the creation of a more secure, democratic, and prosperous world for the benefit of the American people and the international community

---

EDUCATION

Livingstone College – Salisbury, NC
Honorary Doctorate Degree of Humane Letters ***(Hon.D.H.L.)*** • 2004

American Academy McAllister Institute of Funeral Services, Inc. - New York City, NY
Diploma for Principles and Practice of Funeral Services ***(Diploma - Cum Laude)*** • 1976

American University – Washington, DC
Associate in Applied Business ***(A.A.B.)*** • 1975

Henderson Business College – Memphis, TN
Awarded Scholarship
Certification of Completion ***(Diploma)*** • 1944

Booker T. Washington High School – Memphis, TN
General Education Curriculum ***(Diploma)*** • 1943

PROFESSIONAL ASSOCIATIONS

John Wesley African Methodist Episcopal Zion Church – Washington, DC
Member (1945 to Present)
Trustee and Emeritus / Treasurer (1954 to Present)

One of the oldest black churches in the nation's capital emerged in a significant movement of black people to secure self-expression, self-esteem, and freedom in religious worship essential to the prosperity of the spiritual concerns of our colored brethren in general and to the advancement of our Preachers - National Church of Zion Methodism

---

Independent Funeral Director's Association (IFDA)
Member / former Treasurer

A membership association of professional funeral directors and morticians and embalmers whose members and members-at-large are also members of state associations of funeral directors, morticians and embalmers dedicated to promoting the common professional and business interests of its members

*****

National Funeral Director's Association (NFDA)
Member

Provides advocacy, education, information, products, programs and services to help members enhance the quality of service to families

*****

The 100 Black Women in Funeral Services, Inc.
Member / Resolution Recipient

The unwavering support of the perpetuation of the highest ideals of womanhood, service, and achievement in funeral services

*****

Funeral Director's Tenacity Board
Board member

*****

National Association for the Advancement of Colored People (NAACP) – Washington, DC
Life Member

To ensure the political, educational, social, and economic equality of rights of all persons and to eliminate racial hatred and racial discrimination

---

OTHER AFFILIATIONS AND BOARD POSITIONS

Prince Hall Freemason and Eastern Star Charitable Foundation
Board Member

National Capital Child and Family Foundation
Board of Directors
Board Member

University of the District of Columbia – Mortuary Science Program
Funeral Service Board
Board Member

National Graduate University – Washington, DC
Board Member

Tau Gamma Delta Sorority
Supreme Directorate
Member

Lula Williams' A.M.E. Zion Wellness Center – Dinwiddie, VA
Board Member

Alumni Association of Livingstone College – Salisbury, NC
Honorary Member

MAJOR AWARDS

Outstanding Business Award
Century Club of the Business and Professional Women's Club

Business Development Award
Delta Sigma Theta Sorority, Inc.

Outstanding Soror of the Year Award
Tau Gamma Delta Sorority

Outstanding Service to the Business Community
Washington, D.C. Hall of Fame

Outstanding Mortician of the Year
WYCB Radio Broadcast

Outstanding Funeral Director
Independent Funeral Directors Association of Washington, DC

2006-2007 ♦ **Who's Who**
Heritage Registry of Who's Who for 2006-2007

1999, 2000, 2002 and 2003 ♦ **Premier Club Award – Top Firm**
The Leadership Council
Fortis – Assurant Preneed

2003-2004 ♦ **The President's Club Award**
Livingstone College – Salisbury, NC

2004 ♦ **Alumni Hall of Fame**
Livingstone College – Salisbury, NC

2004 ♦ **Victorious Living Award**
Mid-Atlantic II Episcopal District
Bishop Milton A. Williams / Rev. Lula G. Williams

PROFESSIONAL PHILOSOPHY

To demonstrate a love for mankind and a desire to make a difference in God's field here on earth. Be a true visionary, a leader with an unselfish spirit who soars like an eagle above the crowd, always striving to give the very best of self to God and fellow men, which brings about a motto of
"One High Standard of Service"

To continue the quality 50-year career, with a belief that "Service is Friendship in Actions"

I would challenge anyone reading this book who is planning on business endeavors to invest in a quality education or formal training first, and then establish a business plan. Please be sure to identify your target audience and your competitors, and work diligently to become the front-runner in your selected industry by being creative and bold. The Century Club is a great example of this standard.

Over the years, I have found these women to be great informational resources, but most importantly, true friends. With this, I am sharing a birthday tribute that was shared in my honor.

On the Occasion of the 93rd Birthday Celebration for
DR. JULIA P. MARSHALL
At the Alpha Kappa Alpha Sorority House
Washington, D.C.
Sunday, May 26, 2018

I met Dr. Marshall in 1968 at my Aunt's home in Washington, D.C. She has been a very good friend since that day.

Dr. Marshall is a true friend who we all love very much. She is devoutly spiritual, she loves her church and her church family, she is an astute businesswoman, and has many, many, friends. You can see that by the large number of friends gathered here today to celebrate her birthday.

She exhibits strength and calmness in turbulent times and she knows how to maintain equanimity under duress. She is soft spoken, well connected in the community and I think just about "anybody who is somebody" knows Dr. Marshall. But don't let these "soft" words I've been using fool you. She is also a mover and a shaker, can make things happen as she would like them to, and she will stand up for what she knows is right in the face of adversity. She is an advocate for youth and exhibits much perseverance in her efforts to help young people achieve their educational goals. She is my definition of a classy lady and her wisdom guides us all.

Dr. Marshall, we want you to know that all of your sisters in Century Club (a local affiliate of the National Association of Negro Business and Professional Women's Clubs, Inc.) join me today in welcoming all your family members and friends as we celebrate another joyous year. We are already looking forward to next year's party.

Carolyn D. Kornegay
President,
Century Club, NANBPWC, Inc.
Washington, D.C.

Remember to stand on God's promises and offer services that are unique from your competitors; become the trendsetter, and set realistic prices to circumvent defeat before you become established. Proper pricing is imperative, as are effective timelines to keep you focused on your end goal.

Throughout my business career, I have been actively involved in community and civic organizations and have received recognition for my many achievements and support of charitable causes. I have been a member of John Wesley A.M.E. Zion Church for over seventy years and have held various positions of service to the ministry.

My faith has always played an instrumental role in my success. Don't be afraid to reach out to your local churches and to serve in areas needed, because the Lord will bless you. Just as He blessed me. I served as an usher and held various positions in the Body of Christ and still serve with all of my heart and soul because God is worthy to be praised.

7. LIFETIME ACHIEVEMENTS

I am a life member of the NAACP. I am a member and/or a board member of the following:

- The National Association of Minority Political Women, USA
- Tau Gamma Delta Sorority
- The Upper Northwest Business Association
- The Century Club of the National Association of Negro Business and Professional Women's Club
- The Academy of Professional Funeral Service Practice
- The Capitol Hill Kiwanis; the National Funeral Directors
- The Independent Funeral Directors Association
- Board of Directors of the Foundation for Child and Family Development
- The Board of Prince Hall Free Mason and Eastern Star Charitable Foundation of the District of Columbia, Inc.

Community Recognition, Achievements & Awards

I was inducted into the Livingstone College Leaders Hall of Fame for my many years of servant leadership. I received a Legacy Award in Business and was inducted into the District of Columbia Hall of Fame.

Furthermore, I have been honored by numerous organizations and have received many awards honoring my service and success. To name a few, I received:

- The Outstanding Business Award from the Century Club
- The Business Development Award from Delta Sigma Theta, Sorority, Inc. Washington, D.C., Alumnae Chapter
- The Mortician of the Year Award, presented by Lucille B. Miller, Public Relations Officer, WYCS AM Radio
- Outstanding Soror of the Year Award from Tau Gamma Delta Sorority, Inc.
- Outstanding Woman in Funeral Services from the Funeral Directors Association of DC
- Victorious Living Award from the Woman's Home and Overseas Missionary Society Mid-Atlantic II Episcopal District at its Meeting in May 2004

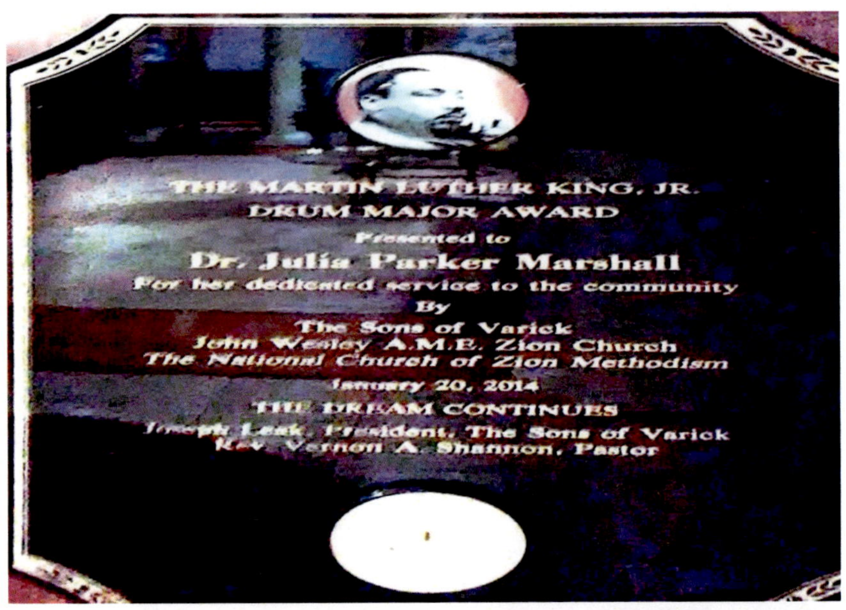
THE MARTIN LUTHER KING, JR.
DRUM MAJOR AWARD
Presented to
Dr. Julia Parker Marshall
For her dedicated service to the community
By
The Sons of Varick
John Wesley A.M.E. Zion Church
The National Church of Zion Methodism
January 20, 2014
THE DREAM CONTINUES
Joseph Leak, President, The Sons of Varick
Rev. Vernon A. Shannon, Pastor

THE DR. JULIA P. MARSHALL
DINING FACILITY

Henderson Business College

Memphis, Tennessee

Be it known, that ________ having completed the prescribed Course in ________ at this College, and having passed satisfactory examinations, is entitled to this

DIPLOMA

awarded by the President and Faculty.

In testimony whereof, we have affixed our signatures this ____ day of ____ in the year of nineteen hundred ____

Sisters 4 Sisters Network, Inc. & BMORENEWS.com

Present

The Black Capitol Awards

to

Dr. Julia Marshall

Marshall-March Funeral Homes

For your commitment to excellence and your undying support of the Black community in the DMV area.

Doni M. Glover
DMGlobal Marketing & PR Creator of BMORENEWS.com

100 BLACK WOMEN OF FUNERAL SERVICE, INC.
THE 2005 JULIA P. MARSHALL
MORTUARY SCHOLARSHIP
SPONSORED BY
JULIA P. MARSHALL
MARSHALL'S FUNERAL HOME
BALTIMORE, MD
ONE HUNDRED BLACK WOMEN OF FUNERAL SERVICE
"Touching the life of others through education."
AUGUST 7, 2005
NFD & MA CONVENTION
NASHVILLE, TN

DR. JULIA P. MARSHALL
HAS BEEN SELECTED AS AN
ORED MEMBER OF
RITAGE REGISTRY
OF
WHO'S WHO
EDITION

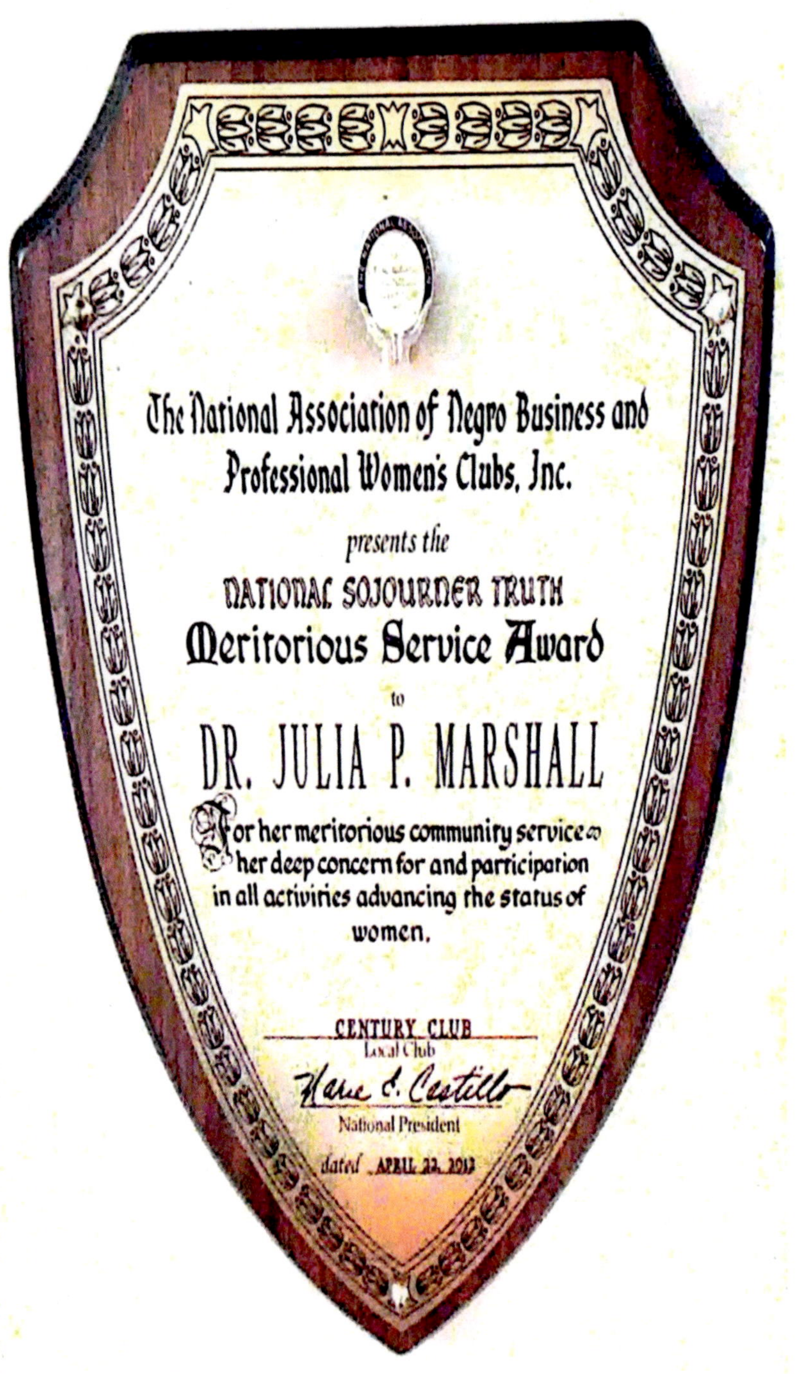
The National Association of Negro Business and Professional Women's Clubs, Inc.
presents the
NATIONAL SOJOURNER TRUTH
Meritorious Service Award
to
DR. JULIA P. MARSHALL
For her meritorious community service & her deep concern for and participation in all activities advancing the status of women.
CENTURY CLUB
Local Club
National President
dated APRIL 22, 2012

The American University

Incorporated by Act of Congress of The United States of America in 1893

In recognition of the successful completion of the prescribed course of study
and by virtue of authority granted by the Congress of the United States of America
has conferred upon

Julia P. Marshall

the degree of

Associate in General Studies

in Social Studies

with all the rights, privileges, responsibilities and honors thereunto appertaining.

In Witness Whereof, the seal of the University and the signatures of duly authorized officers are affixed to this diploma. Given in the City of Washington, District of Columbia, this eighteenth day of May, in the year of Our Lord nineteen hundred and seventy-five.

Chairman of the Board of Trustees

President of the University

Dean, College of Continuing Education

Dean of the College of Public Affairs

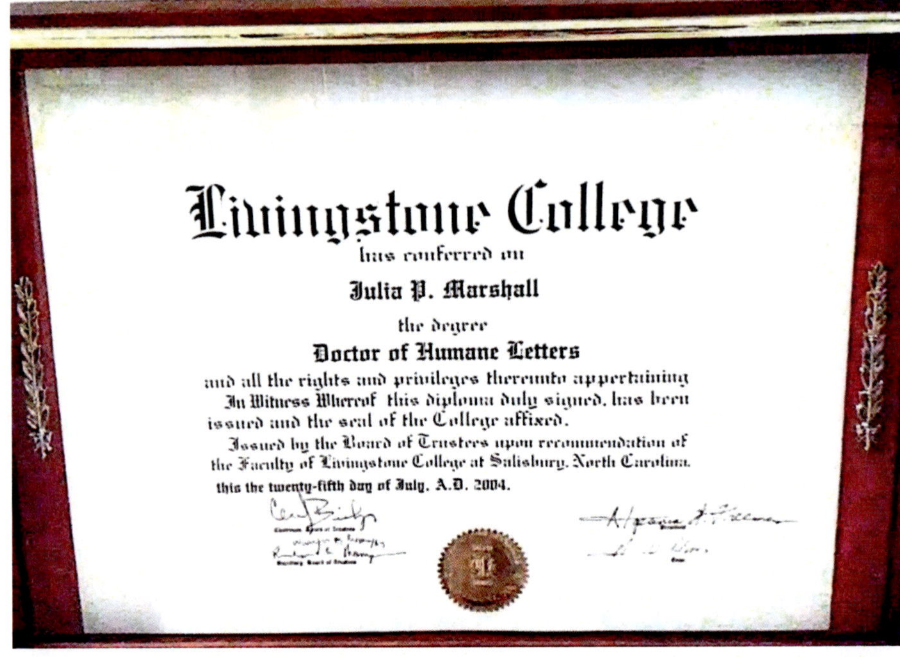

Livingstone College

has conferred on

Julia P. Marshall

the degree

Doctor of Humane Letters

and all the rights and privileges thereunto appertaining
In Witness Whereof this diploma duly signed, has been issued and the seal of the College affixed.
Issued by the Board of Trustees upon recommendation of the Faculty of Livingstone College at Salisbury, North Carolina,
this the twenty-fifth day of July, A.D. 2004.

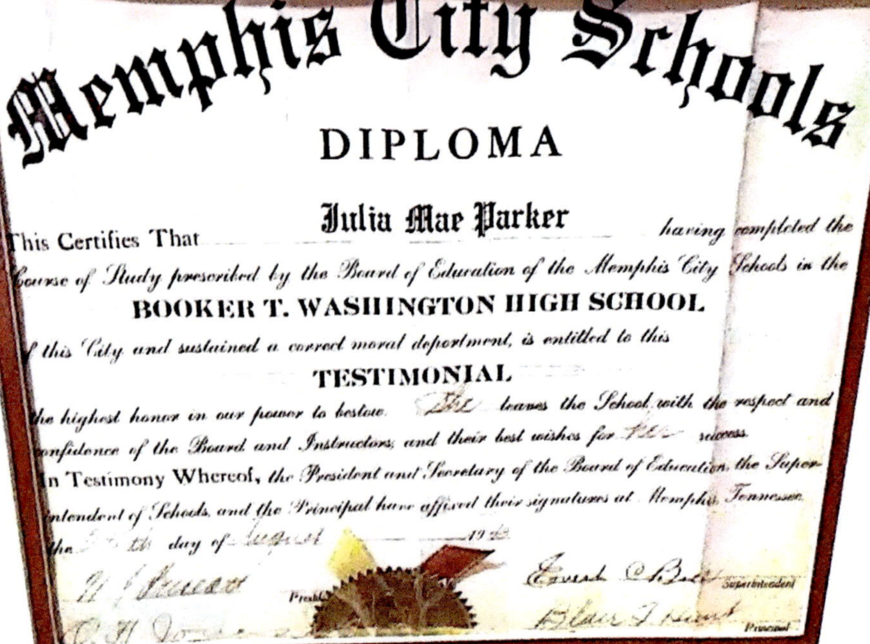

Memphis City Schools

DIPLOMA

This Certifies That Julia Mae Parker having completed the ourse of Study prescribed by the Board of Education of the Memphis City Schools in the

BOOKER T. WASHINGTON HIGH SCHOOL

f this City and sustained a correct moral deportment, is entitled to this

TESTIMONIAL

he highest honor in our power to bestow. She leaves the School with the respect and onfidence of the Board and Instructors, and their best wishes for her success.
In Testimony Whereof, the President and Secretary of the Board of Education, the Superintendent of Schools, and the Principal have affixed their signatures at Memphis, Tennessee, the [illegible] day of August 19[illegible]

President Superintendent Principal

The
100 Black Women in Funeral Service, Inc.

Resolution

Be it hereby known to all that the
100 Black Women In Funeral Service, Inc.
acknowledges with gratitude
the unwavering support of the perpetuation of the
highest ideals of womanhood, service and achievement
by:

Dr. Julia P. Marshall

The entire membership extends
best wishes on this memorable occasion
and directs this resolution be presented on
this 28th day of May 2005.

Doretha Hector
Doretha Hector, CFSP, CPC, Founder, Chief Executive Officer

Mary Winston
Mary Winston, Chairman of the Board

Eleanor Starks
Eleanor Starks, CFSP, Founder, Executive Director

TAU GAMMA
DELTA SORORITY, INC
XI CHAPTER
Honors
JULIA P. MARSHALL

The State of Maryland

Governor of the State of Maryland, to

DR. JULIA P. MARSHALL, Greetings:

Be it Known That on behalf of the citizens of this State,

in recognition of the love and devotion you have always given to your family and friends… with congratulations and sincere best wishes on the occasion of your 80th birthday celebration; and as the people of Maryland join together with your many admirers in expressing our great respect and appreciation for the wonderful difference you have made in the lives of all who have had the privilege and honor of knowing you,

we are pleased to confer upon you this

Governor's Citation

Given [illegible]
[illegible] 28th [illegible] May
[illegible] and five

Governor

Lt. Governor

Secretary of State

A Proclamation

PRINCE GEORGE'S COUNTY MARYLAND

WHEREAS, the Office of the County Executive for Prince George's County, Maryland wishes to recognize the 80th birthday of Dr. Julia P. Marshall and honor her on this significant day in her life; and

WHEREAS, this birthday is indeed a very special occasion and a milestone in the journey of life; and

WHEREAS, birthdays are a time to reflect on the past and to contemplate the future; on this special occasion, as you are surrounded by family and friends from near and far, you are wished a joyous celebration, and may you be blessed with many more birthdays!

NOW, THEREFORE, I, JACK B. JOHNSON, COUNTY EXECUTIVE FOR PRINCE GEORGE'S COUNTY, MARYLAND, do hereby recognize and proclaim the 28th day of May 2005, as a day of celebration and recognition of the 80th birthday of Dr. Julia P. Marshall.

FURTHER, I extend best wishes for much happiness.

Jack B. Johnson

COUNTY EXECUTIVE

Rising
Rest

Josephine Humble Kyles
Woman of the Year Award 2007
Is Presented to
Julia P. Marshall
For Her Unselfish
Dedication to the Life
Sunday November
John Wesley A.M.E. Zion
Washington

THE WHITE HOUSE

WASHINGTON

May 12, 2011

Dr. Julia P. Marshall
c/o Mr. Henry Marrow
4217 Ninth Street, N.W.
Washington, DC 20011

Dear Dr. Marshall:

We are pleased to join your family and friends in wishing you all the best on your birthday.

You have witnessed great milestones in our Nation's history, and your generation has shown the courage to persevere through moments of uncertainty and challenge. Your story is an important part of the American narrative, and we hope you will look back with joy and pride on the many contributions and memories made over the course of your life.

As you celebrate this special occasion, we wish you health and happiness in the years ahead.

Sincerely,

Michelle Obama

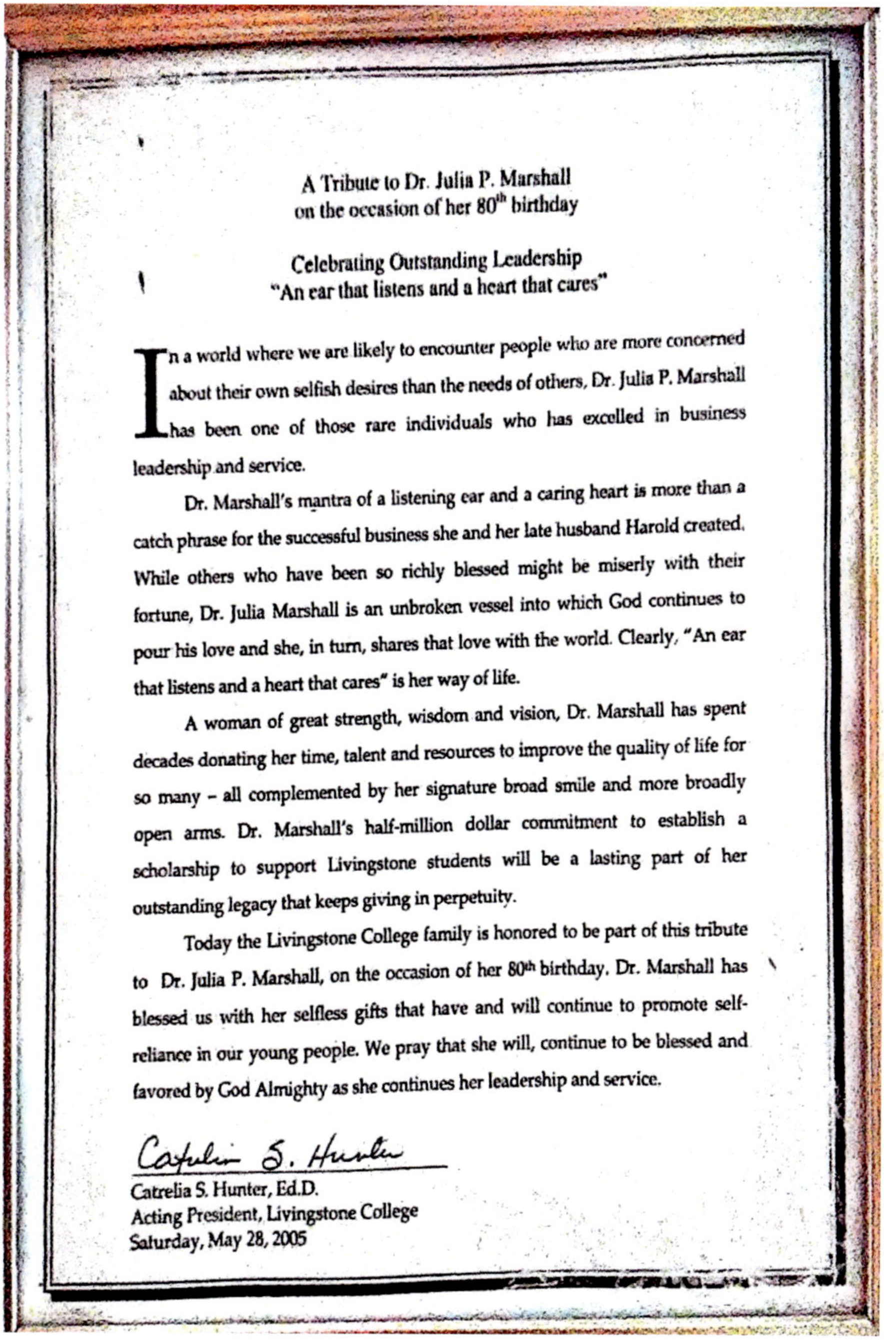

A Tribute to Dr. Julia P. Marshall
on the occasion of her 80th birthday

Celebrating Outstanding Leadership
"An ear that listens and a heart that cares"

In a world where we are likely to encounter people who are more concerned about their own selfish desires than the needs of others, Dr. Julia P. Marshall has been one of those rare individuals who has excelled in business leadership and service.

Dr. Marshall's mantra of a listening ear and a caring heart is more than a catch phrase for the successful business she and her late husband Harold created. While others who have been so richly blessed might be miserly with their fortune, Dr. Julia Marshall is an unbroken vessel into which God continues to pour his love and she, in turn, shares that love with the world. Clearly, "An ear that listens and a heart that cares" is her way of life.

A woman of great strength, wisdom and vision, Dr. Marshall has spent decades donating her time, talent and resources to improve the quality of life for so many – all complemented by her signature broad smile and more broadly open arms. Dr. Marshall's half-million dollar commitment to establish a scholarship to support Livingstone students will be a lasting part of her outstanding legacy that keeps giving in perpetuity.

Today the Livingstone College family is honored to be part of this tribute to Dr. Julia P. Marshall, on the occasion of her 80th birthday. Dr. Marshall has blessed us with her selfless gifts that have and will continue to promote self-reliance in our young people. We pray that she will, continue to be blessed and favored by God Almighty as she continues her leadership and service.

Catrelia S. Hunter

Catrelia S. Hunter, Ed.D.
Acting President, Livingstone College
Saturday, May 28, 2005

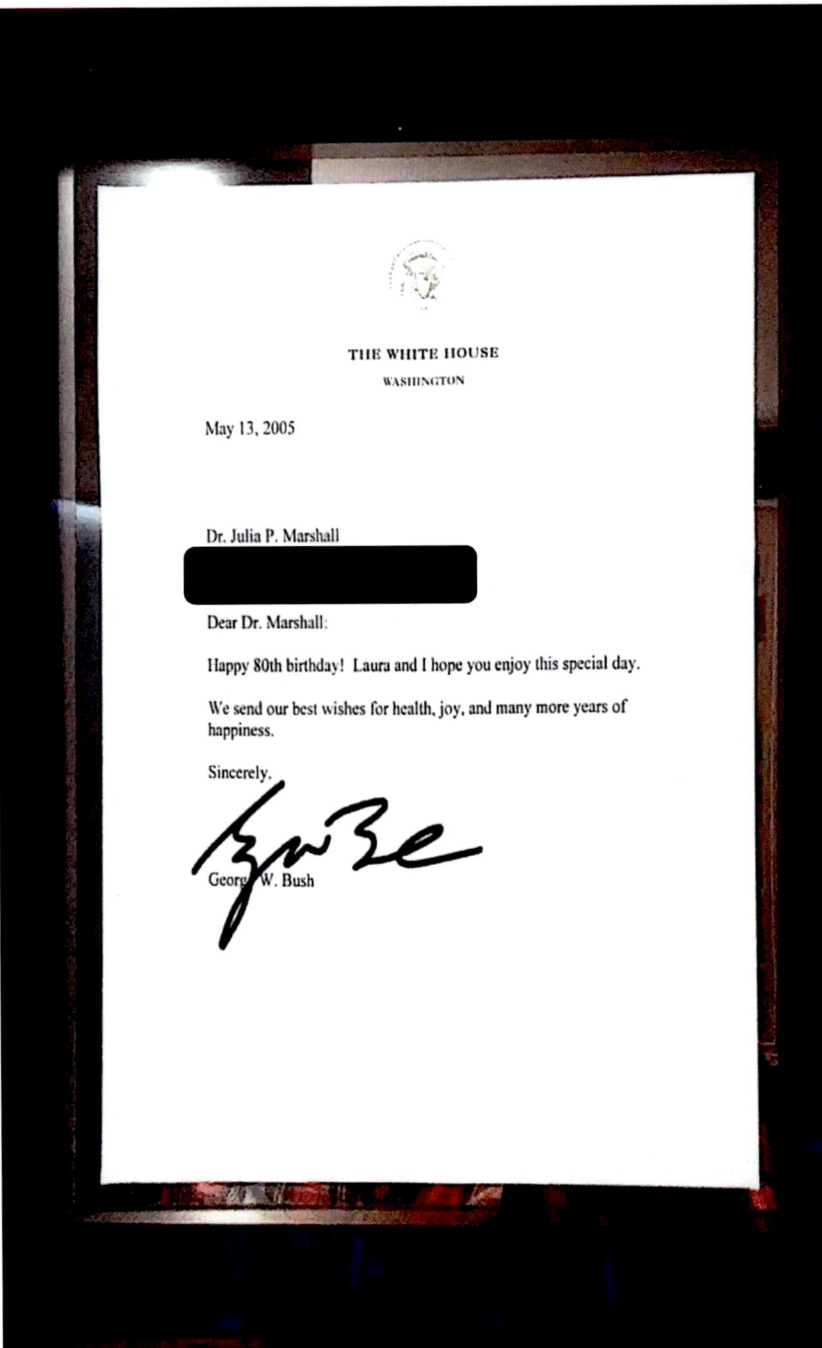

THE WHITE HOUSE

WASHINGTON

May 13, 2005

Dr. Julia P. Marshall

Dear Dr. Marshall:

Happy 80th birthday! Laura and I hope you enjoy this special day.

We send our best wishes for health, joy, and many more years of happiness.

Sincerely,

George W. Bush

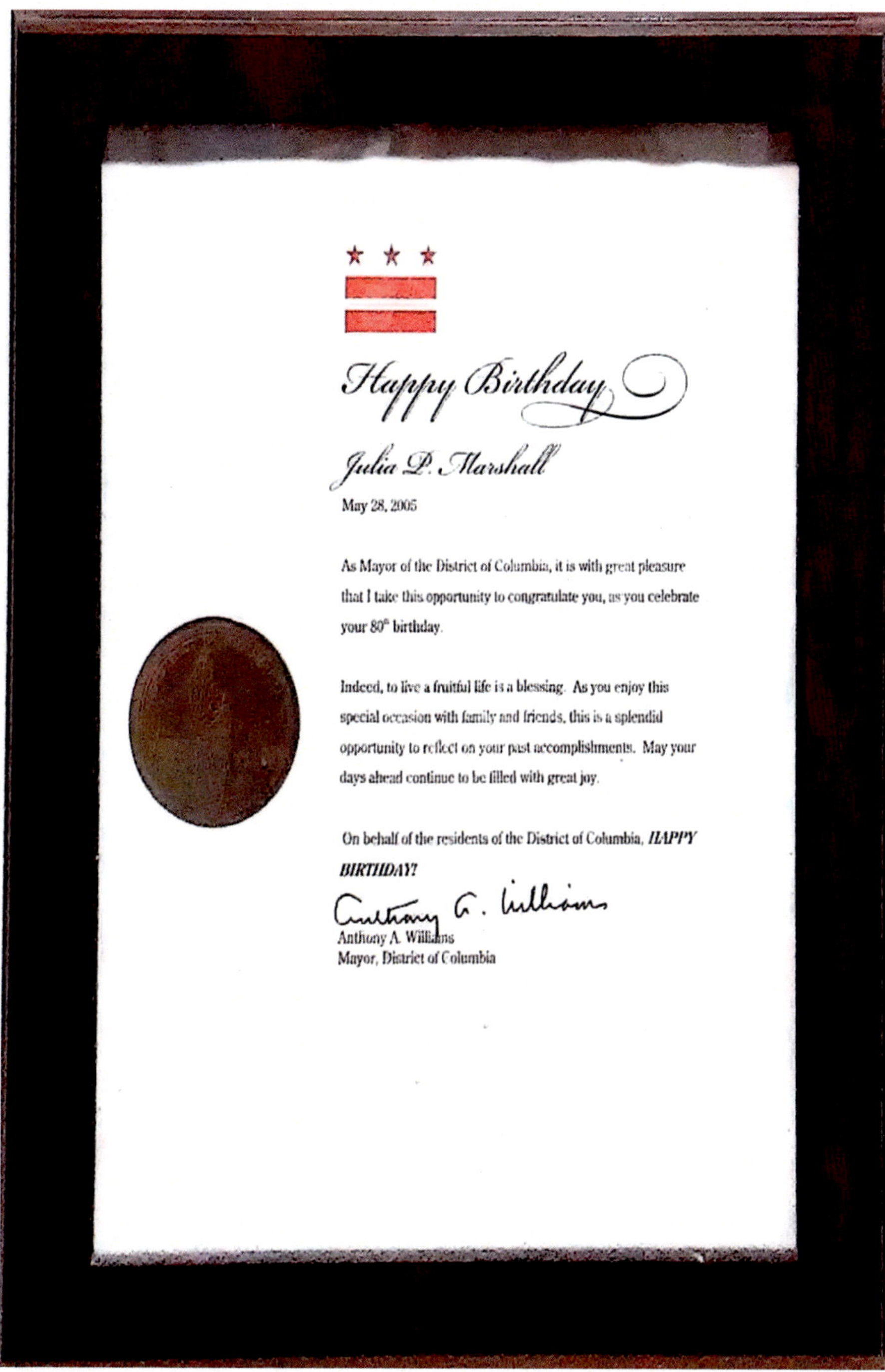

Happy Birthday

Julia P. Marshall

May 28, 2005

As Mayor of the District of Columbia, it is with great pleasure that I take this opportunity to congratulate you, as you celebrate your 80th birthday.

Indeed, to live a fruitful life is a blessing. As you enjoy this special occasion with family and friends, this is a splendid opportunity to reflect on your past accomplishments. May your days ahead continue to be filled with great joy.

On behalf of the residents of the District of Columbia, ***HAPPY BIRTHDAY!***

Anthony A. Williams
Mayor, District of Columbia

COUNCIL OF THE DISTRICT OF COLUMBIA
WASHINGTON, D.C. 20004
www.dccouncil.washington.dc.us
Office: (202) 724-8052
Fax: (202) 724-8120

ADRIAN M. FENTY
Councilmember - Ward 4
Democrat

Chair
Committee on Human Services
Committee Member
Government Operations
Public Works and the Environment
Consumer and Regulatory Affairs

Best Wishes &
Congratulations to
Dr. Julia P. Marshall
As You Celebrate Your
80th Birthday!

May 28, 2005

On behalf of the residents of Ward 4, I wish for you all the best and congratulations as you celebrate your 80th Birthday. Although I can only imagine the many experiences you have had, the milestones you have witnessed and the barriers you have overcome, I would like to acknowledge this special day, paying tribute to your wisdom and your grace and wishing you many, many more birthdays.

May the Lord continue to bless you. Again, congratulations as you celebrate your 80th Birthday.

Sincerely,

Adrian M. Fenty
Councilmember, Ward 4

COUNCIL OF THE DISTRICT OF COLUMBIA

WASHINGTON, D. C. 20004

LINDA W. CROPP
Chairman

"HAPPY 80th BIRTHDAY!"

Dr. JULIA P. MARSHALL

MAY 28, 2005

On behalf of the Council of the District of Columbia and our residents, I take great pleasure in wishing you a very "Happy 80th Birthday!" From your birth in 1925, the world has been in constant change. I am certain you have witnessed and achieved a great deal for your family and your loved ones over the past century. In your birth year Calvin Coolidge was the President of the United States and the Chrysler Corporation was founded. You have undoubtedly achieved a great deal and witnessed many of the great moments in history. But I am particularly impressed that your family and friends have deemed you worthy of a celebration. I do too!

Again, I wish you a wonderful "80th Birthday Celebration." I hope that you thoroughly enjoy yourself on this very special day.

Sincerely,

Linda W. Cropp
Chairman

HOUSE OF REPRESENTATIVES
WASHINGTON, D.C. 20515

ELEANOR HOLMES NORTON
DISTRICT OF COLUMBIA

May 28, 2005

HAPPY BIRTHDAY!

To

Dr. Julia P. Marshall

I am pleased to join your family and friends in honoring you on the occasion of your **80th Birthday**! In noting this significant milepost, we acknowledge both the wisdom and experience you have gained through the years. May your birthday include an opportunity to reinforce the importance of spiritual growth, family, and community.

You have my warmest and best wishes. **HAPPY BIRTHDAY!**

Sincerely,

Eleanor H. Norton

Eleanor Holmes Norton

TO:

Dr. Julia Parker-Marshall

FROM:

Rev. J. C. Clark, B. A., B. S., M. A., M. S., M. Ed., M. B. A., M. Div., D. Min., Ph.D.

2122 – 56th Street
P. O. Box 2530
Lubbock, TX 79408-2530
(806)-744-5727
(806)-577-5823

Washington D.C.
Hall of Fame Society, In
WASHINGTON D.C
Hall of Fa
COGNIZING LE

The Parker Family from coast to coast salutes Dr. Julia P. Marshall
for being named to the **2007 Living Legends List** to receive the
"2007 Mary Louise Winston Pyramid of Success Award"

Congratulations, Dr. Julia P. Marshall on your outstanding recognition from the One Hundred Black Women in Funeral Services Organization. You have been a lightening rod which is demonstrated by your success. Your life reads like a good book which reveals the content of your character, your entrepreneurial-ship, your spirit as a philanthropist and community activist have been outstanding. There are so many chapters that capture the blueprint for your success. The family thanks you for the rich legacy and the roots you've established for all the generations to witness. We are so proud of you and all your accomplishments. We hope you keep accelerating because we're waiting to read the next chapter of the dynasty you built through dedication and perseverance. You took the road less traveled and God has blessed you for not only who you are but for being the champion and embracing causes that has enriched the lives of others.

Your generosity of giving and your quiet demeanor accentuates your beauty as the Queen of our family. You are as electrifying, as you are beautiful. We thank the One Hundred Black Women for acknowledging you because there is no greater honor than being recognized by not only your own kind but by your own gender.

We hope God continue to Bless You -

Love,

The Parker Family
From
Coast to Coast

Memphis, Tennessee; Matteson, Illinois; Chicago, Illinois; Steilacoom, Washington; Oakland, California; Richfield, Minnesota; Lithonia, Georgia; Detroit, Michigan; Minneapolis, Minnesota; Hopkins, Minnesota; Sacramento, California; Fontana, California; Cleveland, Ohio; Little Elm, Texas; Los Angeles, California

Chicago, Illinois:

Eula Stokes; Patricia Upton; Robert, Tiffany & Family; Joseph, Mandisa & Family; Michael Upton

Minneapolis, Minnesota:

Walter, Josephine & Family

Seattle, Washington:

Lavender Parker & Ruby Jewitt

Dr. Julia P. Marshall

Long Time Director of Marshall's Funeral Homes is Honored with Th Julia P. Marshall Humanitarian Hall

On Sunday July 29th John Wesley Methodist Episcopal Zion Church named the second floor of their beautifully expanded Parish Hall The Julia P. Marshall Humanitarian Hall.

In a beautiful Naming Ceremony, presided over by Rev. Vernon Shannon, beautiful songs were sung by Mrs. Rosalyn Murphy-Jenkins and Reamer Shedrick. Tributes were given by:

Mrs. Linda Roseman Pettaway, Preacher's Steward:

Proverbs 22: 1 says, "A good name is rather to be chosen than great riches, and loving favor rather than silver and god." "I believe that we should be honored that this space will be known as the Julia P. Marshall Humanitarian Hall."

Mr. Cleanie Murphy Jr., Chair of the Historical Society Exp Committee:

"John Wesley has blessed through Dr. Mars for more than 12 year Marshall was a Sunday Sc

continued on page

Article and photo credits unknown; special thanks to the author (unknown).

Dr. Julia P. Marshall Named to Heritage Registry

Photos by Maurice G. Fitzgerald

Dr. Julia P. Marshall and her late husband, Harold Marshall, have both been included in the forthcoming 2006-2007 edition of the *Heritage Registry of Who's Who*™.

This New York-based biographical publication selects and distinguishes individuals throughout North America who have attained a recognizable degree of success in their field of endeavor, thereby contributing to the growth of their industry. Biographical profiles highlight each selected member. Inclusion is by invitation only. The volume will be available at the Library of Congress and other libraries.

Marshall is known

success of the funeral home she established with her husband in 1968, building it from the ground up. The business now has two loca-

Washington

D.C. and one in Suitland, Maryland.

Mrs. Marshall has dedicated herself to preparing families for the hereafter and is deeply committed to living out Harold's business philosophy —"Service Is Friendship in Action." She continues that philosophy to this day.

In addition, Julia Marshalls has always been known for service to her community, both through her church and other institutions, and directly to community members.

Publisher J.C. Cooke and *The Washington Sun* family extend congratulations to Dr. Marshall on this well-deserved honor bestowed on her and her late husband.

Article and photo credits unknown; special thanks to The Star of Zion (author unknown).

Dr. Julia P. Marshall Inducted into the Democracy Hall of Fame International

Long Time Director of Marshalls Funeral Homes

he International Graduate versity's Democracy Hall of e International inducted a inguished business woman, Julia P. Marshall, in a festive ier ceremony. Dr. Julia P. rshall, a successful business, leader of Washington, DC, on Saturday, September 25. The theme of this special program was the essential role of private enterprise in the development and maintenance of democracies in the world. In addition to Dr. Marshall's address during which she shared her wisdom learned from establishing and operating a highly praised business. Presiding during the induction was Chairman of the Industrial Bank of Washington, Mr. Clinton W. Chapman, Esq. Dr. Jimmy R. Jenkins, Sr.. President of Livingstone College and Dr. Walter E. Boek, President of International Graduate University.

The program began with a reception in the Hall on 13th

continued on page 5

Article and photo credits and special thanks to Washington Sun (author unknown).

May 2

Hall of Fame Society presents annual Legacy Awards

By "Mickey" Thompson

The Washington Hall of Fame Society presented it's fifth Annual Legacy Awards on April 18 at the Marriott Wardman Park Hotel.

Awardees included Julia Marshall, Legacy Award in business; Jerry Phillips, Legacy Award in communications; Kent Amos, Legacy Award in community development; Charles H. Atherton, Legacy Award in cultural arts; Vera White accepted the Legacy Award in educat Margie Scott, Legacy Award in health; Judge Julia Cooper Mack, Legacy Award in law; the Rev. James O. West, Legacy Award in religic Dr. Zaki Sherif, Legacy Award in science and technology and Frieda Valentine, Legacy Award for sports.

The Regional Achievent Award was given to Lacey Wilson Jr. of the Florida Avenue Grill and, last but not least, the Diamond Legacy Award was given to Chief Judge Eugene Hamilton. Four posthumous awards were given to: Dr. Alfred Goldson, accepted by his widow, Amy Goldson, attorney; developer, Theodore Hagans, accepted by his daughter, Michele Hagen; Kimi O. Gray, the founder of the Colleg Here We Come program, and the Rev. Ernest Gibson, former pastor of First Rising Mount Zion Baptist Church.

Article & photo credits unknown; special thanks to the article producer – Mickey Thompson.

KIWANIS CLUB OF CAPITOL HILL

The members of the Kiwanis Club of Capitol Hill would like to extend our congratulations to fellow Kiwanian, Dr. Julia P. Marshall for her induction into the Democracy Hall of Fame International.

Dr. Marshall was elected to this honor by the Board of Governors of the International Graduate University, not only because of her abilities and determination to make a success of the business she and her late husband founded, but also because of her many kindnesses, as exemplified by her membership in the Capitol Hill Kiwanis Club.

She also has been generous in funding scholarships and assistance for others to obtain their education in an era when this is an essential prerequisite to success.

Congratulations Julia!

In Kiwanis,

Freeman Wise, President

The Washington Sun • April 29, 2004 • Page 3

Legacies of Role-Model Washingtonians Recognized at Hall of Fame Ceremony

AWARDS (from p. 1)

vineyard. We have provided a vehicle to showcase our history and talent, but, more important, to remember those who were pioneers. It is with great pride that I congratulate our fifth group of inductees into the Washington, D.C. Hall of Fame, class of 2004."

WASHINGTON, D.C. HALL OF FAME: 2004 INDUCTEES

Business
Julia P. Marshall

Communications
Jerry Phillips

Community Development
Kent Amos

Cultural Arts
Charles H. Atherton

Education
Vera M. White

Health
Margie Scott Word

Law
Judge Julia P. Cooper Mack

Politics
Clifford L. Alexander, Jr.

Religion
Reverend James O. West, Jr.

Science/Technology
Dr. Zaki Sherif

Sports
Fred L. Valentine

Diamond Legacy Award
Judge Eugene N. Hamilton.

Regional Award
Lacy Wilson, Florida Avenue Grill

Posthumous Awards
Theodore Hagans • Reverend Ernest R. Gibson • Dr. Alfred Goldson • Kimi Gray

The Hall of Fame Awardees are selected by a panel of recognized experts in Business, Communication, Community Development, Cultural Arts, Eduction, Health, Law, Politics, Religion, Science/Technology, and Sports.

Recognition by the D.C. Hall of Fame is an esteemed tribute to Washington, D.C. residents who have distinguished themselves in the city in many areas of professional service for at least the last decade. Candidates for this honor had to be nominated by another party' self-nomination was not allowed.

Criteria for selection include:

- **Residency:** Each nominee must be a resident of the city and have resided here continuously for at least ten years.
- **Pioneering Work/Experience:** Contributions and work accomplishment that brought the nominee national or international recognition.
- **Organizational Leadership:** Judges considered all the organizations or companies in which the nominee held or holds leadership positions.
- **Professional Achievement:** The judges also took into account the nominee's professional accomplishments.
- **Scholarship:** Publications and writings, educational awards, inventions, and exceptional performances are also criteria.
- **Community Leadership:** All nominees must be actively involved in the community.

The Legacy Awards Program was held at the Marriott Wardman Park Hotel in Northwest D.C. The black tie event, attended by many local luminaries, included a silent auction. The Hall of Fame Scholarship was awarded to District of Columbia students, and a contribution was made to the Washington, D.C. African American Museum, Inc. a 501(c)(3) organization.

Nominations for the 2005 Hall of Fame Legacy Awards are due by October 28, 2004, and remain active for two years. Self-nominations are not accepted. Nominees must be at least 35 years of age and meet the above criteria. For an official nomination form, visit <www.washingtondchalloffame.org>, call 202/673-6545, fax to 202/671-0653, or write the Washington D.C. Hall of Fame Society, Inc., P.O. Box 73065, Washington, D.C. 20056-3065.

Article credits and special thanks to Washington Sun (author unknown).

100 Black Women of Funeral Service
Certificate of Membership
ONE HUNDRED BLACK WOMEN OF FUNERAL SERVICE
Dr. Julia Marshall
A Woman of Distinction in the Funeral Service Profession that Exemplifies; Dynamic Leadership, Efficient Management Skills, Unparalleled Vision and Insight and the Highest Standards of Professionalism and Integrity.
You are hereby granted the honor, rights and privileges pertaining to the membership of the National Association of "100 Black Women of Funeral Service."
Elleanor Davis Starks, CFSP
Founder - Executive Director
Dorotha Hector, CFSP-CPC
President and CEO
Leadership

January 9, 2009

Greetings,

The change has come!

Please find enclosed your American Music Inaugural Ball ticket(s) along with a copy of the confirmation receipt for your records.

Tickets purchased for the indoor widescreen viewing of President-elect Barack Obama's Oath of Office, Presidential Address and Inaugural Parade (breakfast and/or brunch) on Tuesday, January 20th, will be available at the Marriott Wardman Park Hotel Will Call Desk located at 2660 Woodley Road, N.W., Washington, D.C. These tickets will be available for pick-up beginning Sunday, January 18th through Monday, January 19th. On January 20th, tickets will be available one-hour prior to the start of the event. A photo ID is required to pick-up tickets.

Please note that you must be seated for the viewing by 11:30 a.m. NO EXCEPTIONS. No one will be allowed to enter the Maryland Room between 11:45 am – 12:05 pm to view the Oath of Office for the Vice President-elect and President-elect after the ceremony has begun. The doors will reopen at 12:05 pm for the viewing of the Presidential Address and Inaugural Parade.

Thank you for joining the American Music Inaugural Ball & Events Committee to celebrate this historic event.

Enclosures: (1) Confirmation Receipt
(2) Event Ticket(s)

Dionne & Friends Foundation, Inc. ♫ 5 Thomas Circle, N.W., 5th Floor ♫ Washington, D.C. 20005 ♫ (202) 332-0072
www.AmericanMusicInauguralBalls.com

PRESIDENT BARACK OBAMA

Dear Dr. Marshall,

As a gesture of my gratitude for your friendship and support, I hope you will accept the enclosed special piece of art which celebrates my second Inauguration.

This year's inaugural ceremonies took place on Dr. Martin Luther King, Jr. Day, a day on which the nation gathers together to celebrate a man who stirred our collective conscience … whose life and work ultimately made our union more perfect.

Without his words, his actions, and his sacrifice, we might not have had the courage to come as far as we have. Because of him, new doors of opportunity swung open for a new generation … for me, for my children, and for future generations whose potential we cannot even begin to imagine.

The print enclosed, and the day it depicts, is particularly important to me because of all it represents: the progress we as a nation have made in our short history together … and the promise of a future, even brighter than the years before.

Dr. Marshall, you and I have accomplished a lot together since I first took office in 2009. A decade of war is now ending, and an economic recovery is underway. We enacted historic health insurance reform, and passed tough new regulations for financial companies to protect consumers.

Yet you and I both know the challenges we have overcome together haven't come easy. We have come a long way together … but our work is not finished.

We must work together to ensure that prosperity truly rests upon the broad shoulders of a strong middle class … that no citizen is forced to wait hours to exercise their right to vote … and that hopeful young immigrants who still see America as a land of opportunity are welcomed into our country.

I need you by my side as I work to fulfill the basic promise that no matter what you look like, no matter where you came from, and no matter your station in life, this country is a place where you can make it if you try.

Thank you for all you have done for the Democratic Party … and for me. We have much more to achieve over the coming four years, and I hope I can continue to count on your ongoing support.

Sincerely,

President Barack Obama

265800-77

2014 Commemorative Presidential Print

Presented to Dr. Julia Marshall

By President Barack Obama and the Democratic National Committee

Dr. Julia P. Marshall Awarded The Josephine Humble Kyles Woman of the Year Award

Photo by Maurice G. Fitzgerald

(left to right) Rev. Vernon A. Shannon, Pastor, John Wesley AME Zion Chuch, Dr. Julia P. Marshall and Willie Coleman

On Sunday November 11, 2007, at the John Wesley AME Zion Church's Women's Day Celebration, Dr. Julia P. Marshall was awarded the Josephine Humble Kyles Woman of the Year Award.

The Theme of the day was Christian Women Ambassadors for Christ. The guest speaker was the Rev. Dr. Mildred "Bonnie" Hines, Pastor of First African Methodist Episcopal Zion Church in Los Angeles, CA.

The purpose of the award is to acknowledge a woman that is a member of John Wesley AME Zion Church for her outstanding contributions to the church and to the community. Dr. Marshall is very actively involved in her community. She's certainly no stranger to honors and recognition. Dr. Marshall has devoted her life to community service and a steadfast devotion to the AME Zion Church while also achieving remarkable success in the business world.

A widely recognized business and community leader, she described how she has successfully continued to manage the business that she and her late husband founded in D.C

She feels fortunate and blessed to help build one of the most successful funeral service businesses in the Washington metropolitan area.

Article credits and special thanks to Washington Sun. Author unknown; photo credits to Maurice Fitzgerald.

8. LOVE ONE ANOTHER

Since you now understand the way that God has blessed my life abundantly, I would like to refer to the Apostle Paul's first letter to the Church of Corinth, a church whose members seemingly did not realize that the church is the body of Christ and can only function as it should when all of its members work together.

The church was divided because there were problems among its members. A group of members who prided themselves on possessing certain spiritual gifts but scorned and downplayed the spiritual gifts of others in an attempt to emphasize and clarify the matter that stemmed a tide of confusion. Paul likens the body of Christ to a human body and pinned the words found in 1 Corinthians 12:12: "For as the body of Christ is one, and hath many members, and all the members of that body being many, are one body, so also is Christ."

As I reflect on a theme that I was honored to speak on, during a speaking engagement with my church, "Christian Women United Working for God's Kingdom Building," I would like to share with you what this means to me. I believe this theme suggests that, in spite of the fact that we all come from different neighborhoods and family backgrounds, different professions with various titles, have various degrees of God-given talents and different levels of spiritual maturity, you should not permit discord to deter your willingness to unite and to work together for the causes of Christ.

Please commit to serving your church leadership with humble acts of gratitude, because we have an obligation to love our churches with the love of God, therefore meeting its needs just as the Lord meets ours. I believe that if we revere the way the Lord nurtures and cares for us while we serve in ministry, it will change the dynamic of the way we love one another as members of the body of Christ.

Call to Action

Are you willing to unite and work together for Christ?

I feel confident in saying that working together is not always easy; in fact, it requires extra effort to understand and consider the desires and needs of others without compromising your obligations to Jesus Christ.

If you are really willing to unite together for Christ, you must be willing to empty yourself individually of excessive self-concern and make room for the interests of others in the means of selfless service, without compromising the will of God concerning your individual path.

To make it plain, in instances where we volunteer, this does not make you less qualified than if you receive compensation for that same service; hence, when we give of ourselves for Kingdom building, we should do this with high standards because it is only what we do for Christ that will last.

Christian women must build one another up and bear one another's burdens; we must be receptive to one another's ideas and be willing not to engage in behaviors that cause division and disunity in the Body of Christ; and we must demonstrate our trust and belief in God's words by implementing it in the way we treat one another.

In Philippians 2:3, the Holy Scripture tells us: "Let nothing be done through strife or vain-glory; but in lowliness of mind, let each esteem others better than themselves." Every so often, we must conduct self-assessment to make sure that we are presenting ourselves as representations of Christ on Earth. We must operate in the love of God with the willingness to let go of the records of wrong when loving one another so that we can love healthily and advance the Kingdom of God.

In the fourth chapter of Paul's letter to the Philippians, we find an account of conflict between two women, named Euodias and Syntyche. Both women were described by Paul as "those who labored side by side with him." Theologians have suggested that they may have been deaconesses. Their conflict appears not to be theological but personal.

Sister Euodias and Sister Syntyche clearly had differences over petty matters, but which were serious enough to hinder and endanger the unity of the Philippians and which caused Paul to write: "I beseech Euodias and beseech Syntyche that they be in the same mind in the Lord."

In our familial and romantic relationships, we need men whose hearts are on fire for God. Christian boys and girls must have the faith of Shadrach, Meshach, and Abednego, who will not bow down to idolatry.

What lessons from the life of Jesus impressed you regarding women in the Gospel, and in what ways are you preparing to advance the Kingdom of God, if you are not already prepared? Consider the woman with the issue of blood, who believed that if she could touch the hem of Jesus' garment that she would be made whole. Ponder on the bravery and courage of Esther, the queen, whose name means "star." Remember Prophetess Deborah, who was a judge, who became the Mother of Israel; and last but not least, think about Ruth, whose name means "friend," and focus on the significant impact of ways that friendships attract unforeseen blessings.

It pays to serve Jesus: it pays every day, it pays every step of the way. I learned this especially when I was honored with an Honorary Doctorate of Humane Letters from Livingstone college, a 126-year-old institution affiliated with the African Methodist Episcopal Zion Church. I was honored for doing what I loved, and I am very grateful to have been able to be a blessing touching the lives of so many families.

This book is written in God's love. I am fulfilling my post-retirement dream. It is never too late to achieve your goals or to remind family members of your love, faithfulness, and dedication to them and success, as well.

God has graced me with time to spend with you and my church family, and I appreciate your love, kind words, respect, and most importantly the memories that we create together.

A Word of Prayer

I pray that you will be encouraged and inspired by my life in some way, because the Parker family can do all things through Christ. He is our strength.

Earlier, I shared that I have been a blessed member of John Wesley African American Methodist Episcopal Zion Church for over seventy years and that, during this time, I have served as a Sunday-schoolteacher, an usher, treasurer of the Church, trustee, and as a member of a host of organizations.

I expounded on my endeavors in other sections of this book and highlighted the significant role that servant leadership has played in my life; I also shared the background to my life achievements and provided tributes to individuals who have labored with me in love and in service.

My life journey shows that with faith, all things are possible. God is faithful to those who believe and work hard to achieve. Stand on God's promises and remember to bless someone with the Love of God, because you never know who might need it.

Mrs. Wilhelma J. Bishop

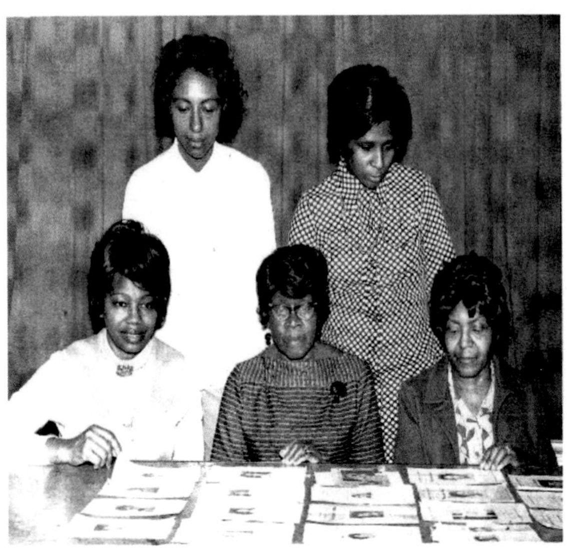

Pictured above: The John Wesley African Methodist Episcopal Zion Church Queen Search Committee, where we honored 25 young ladies and awarded them John Wesley Queens.

Over sixty-two years ago, I supported Mrs. More D. Tolbert in the fulfillment of her dream. Together, we developed a contest for young women of John Wesley Church to compete for the title of "Miss John Wesley."

The overall goal was to recognize women of tremendous talent willing to sacrifice for the causes of God. This program was a means of keeping young women engaged in the Church by encouraging them to use their gifts. We succeeded, and I am honored that we were able to create an amazing program that blessed the lives of many women. We created a self-validating experience that caused the winners of the pageant to earn their right to be a "Queen" of service in the House of God.

John Wesley African Methodist Episcopal Zion Church
National Church of Zion Methodism
1615th Street, NW Washington, DC 20009
202-667-3824
Rev. Vernon A. Shannon, Pastor

April 16, 2006

The Reverend Dr. Mary E. Ivey, President and Founder
Maine Avenue, Inc.
Maine Avenue Ministries
6120 Oregon Avenue, NW
Washington, DC 20015-1140

Dear Dr. Ivey:

In honoring and inducting Dr. Julia P. Marshall into the "World Hall of Love" at your Seventh Annual World Spiritual Service Leadership/Scholarship Awards Program, your are really honoring yourselves and one of the most honorable persons of our region and nation..

Dr. Julia P. Marshall, a recipient of the honorary Doctor's Degree from Livingstone College and a recent inductee into the Livingstone College Hall of Fame is a senior member of John Wesley African Methodist Episcopal Zion Church. She has served in various leadership capacities of our church for many years and now serves as a member of our Trustee Board.

In addition to her membership at our Church, Dr. Marshall is also a member of several leading Community organizations of our community and city. Her service to our city has led to her induction into "District of Columbia Hall Fame."

Dr. Marshall, owner of the Marshall's Funeral Home, one of the prominent Funeral Homes of our region and nation, has a heart that reaches widely, and hands that serve people with integrity and dignity. She serves with humility and compassion.

In honoring Dr. Julia P. Marshall, you are honoring a person of faith and commitment and compassion, deepened by the desire to serve God and humankind. Her concern for the youth of the community has been expressed by her determined efforts to support programs and activities that encourage and enrich the youth of our community.

You are blessed to have Dr. Julia P. Marshall accept your invitation to become your honoree.
CONGRATULATIONS!

Sincerely,

Vernon A. Shannon, Pastor

John Wesley A. M. E. Zion Church

National Church of Zion Methodism

1615 14th Street, NW 202-667-3824 Washington, DC 20009

June 4, 2007

Doretha F. Hector, CFSP-CPC
PO Box 916404
Longwood, Florida 32791

Dear Ms. Hector,

The Board of Directors and Officers of the 100 Black Women of Funeral Service Inc., has acted with intelligent application for knowledge in selecting Dr. Julia P. Marshall as the recipient of the Funeral Service "Living Legend Award" at your second annual Academy Awards of Funeral Services to be held on Wednesday, August 1, 2007 during the 70th Annual Convention of the National Funeral Directors and Morticians Association, Inc. in Philadelphia, Pa.

Dr. Julia P. Marshall, a founder with her late husband, and owner of Marshall's Funeral Home, Inc., with locations in Suitland, Md. and Washington is among the most prominent and respected Funeral Homes in the Washington Metropolitan area. Mrs. Marshall has achieved greatness not only through her highly professional funeral services, but also more importantly in her willingness to extend herself in service to humanity.

Mrs. Marshall is generous with her time, reaching out to many of the Washington area's communities and professional organizations. She involves herself in many of the region's activities. She is an active and committed member of The John Wesley African Methodist Episcopal Zion Church, the National Church of Zion Methodism, Washington, DC; where she serves as a trustee and on numerous other boards and committees.

She has been inducted into the, Washington, DC Hall of Fame Society, for her tremendous impact on the growth and development of the District of Columbia and her many contributions which have helped to enhance the quality of life for those whom she has touched. She has established and maintains a high standard of excellence for others to emulate.

She has adopted the motto of the United Negro College Fund believing that, "A MIND IS A TERRIBLE THING TO WASTE." She realizes that the continued advancement of our race and nation is dependent upon the education of our youth. She is a generous supporter of educational endeavors and as a consequence was inducted into the "Livingstone College Hall of Fame" and is the recipient of an Honorary Doctorate Degree from the College.

Dr. Marshall has received in excess of fifty awards and citations from community and professional organizations in recognition of her support. She travels extensively and has visited throughout the United States and the world.

In selecting Dr. Julia P. Marshall to be the recipient of your Funeral Service's "Living Legend Award", you have chosen a woman who embodies the essence of regal womanhood and one whose faith, commitment and compassion is deepened by her desire to serve God and humankind.

Congratulations,

Vernon A. Shannon

Bethel Memorial
African Methodist Episcopal Church
Hazendal

Service of Thanksgiving
&
Welcome Reception
of our
Special guest from the U.S.A.

Wednesday, 20 July 2005.

The Rt. Rev. Samuel Green (Snr): Presiding Bishop
The Rev. Andrew B.G. Lewin: Pastor & Presiding Elder
Dr Julia Parker-Marshall: Guest Speaker, Washington D.C.
Mr. Andrew M.E. Joubert: Organist

Golden Class Reunion Celebration
1958 – 2008

Please come to a Golden Class Reunion Celebration in honor of alumni of Howard University's School of Religion, Class of 1958, including Cecil Bishop and Frederick W. Barnes. Let us mingle and celebrate with them as they observe their 50th anniversary class reunion!

Date: Saturday, May 10, 2008

Time: 3:00 PM – 5:30 PM

Place: The home of Dr. Julia P. Marshall

Washington, DC 20008

CERTIFICATE OF APPRECIATION

is presented to

JULIA MARSHALL

For your outstanding efforts in support of women in ministry

Date **March 8, 1996**

Attest: Kathleen G. Arnold, Interim
Secretary of the District of Columbia

Marion Barry
Mayor

9. LIVINGSTONE COLLEGE

Livingstone College Confers New Honor on Mrs. Julia P. Marshall

Livingston College recently conferred the honorary degree Doctor of Humane Letters on Mrs. Julia P. Marshall (shown above receiving her honorary degree), chief executive officer and owner of Marshall's Funeral Homes. In February 2004, Mrs. Livingstone's highest honors when she was officially inducted into the Livingston College Alumni Hall of Fame.

Livingstone College is located in Salisbury, North Carolina and is a 125-year-old institution of higher learning affiliated with the Zion Church.

The recent honor was conferred upon Mrs. Marshall during a formal ceremony held on July 25 at the John Wesley A.M.E. Zion Church in Washington D.C. and presided over by Dr. Algeania W. Freeman, president of Livingstone College.

Article and photo credits (unknown); special thanks to Washington Sun.

Dr. Marshall Thanks Livingstone College

Even now, I am forever honored for the awards that this amazing academic institution saw fit to grant me. As I have traveled on life's highway, God has showered many blessings upon me, and I am thankful to add all awards and honors acquired to my list of blessings.

In the years ahead, as students come and go, they will have a visual point of reference showing the Marshalls love, concern, and dedication to their academic success. I am blessed to have been allowed to fulfill the vision of myself and my late-husband Harold Marshall by providing a scholarship fund to Livingstone College.

Furthermore, I commend Livingstone College for what it has done to help its students to receive a formal education, regardless of the struggle to accomplish their goals. Education was important to my parents, and likewise, it is important to me and thus it gives me great pleasure to support your education.

The Bible says in Proverbs 9, verse 9: "Give instructions to a wise man, and he will be wiser; teach that man and he will increase in learning.

I remain deeply touched by the naming of the cafeteria in my honor, because it is a blessing that surpasses all others. Thank you, Dr. Julia P. Marshall.

10. JOURNEY OF TRAVEL

REV. ANDREW BENJAMIN GANDHI LEWIN FOR BISHOP 2008
"STILL FOCUSED FOR THE FUTURE"

28th July 2005

Dear Dr Julia,

Grace, Mercy and Peace from God the Father and Our Lord, Jesus Christ.

This missive comes to thank you for blessing us with your presence. Words cannot adequately describe our gratitude to you for your kindness. God most certainly smiled upon us the day He allowed our paths to cross with yours. You will never realise how deeply you have touched the people of Gugulethu. Through your generosity you have given a people who were despondent and despaired, new hope and vision for the future, which, until you came were very bleak. You are indeed an angel sent by God Himself.

Thank you for opening your heart and hand toward us. In due time the building will be erected and will bear witness and testimony for generations to come that a remarkable woman of God, called Julia Parker-Marshall came this way. I will keep you abreast on the building project and its development. I have informed Dr Jim Clark of what transpired at the Thanksgiving and Welcome reception Service we had.

I believe that every person is birthed by God for a purpose. I also believe that it is not by accident or coincidence, but by divine design that God would have me pursue the office of Bishop in our Church. There is a need in the African Methodist Episcopal Church to elect persons from Africa who mirror the culture and diversity of our people. I am one of those persons. Most of the campaign work has to be done in Continental USA. Deep in my heart I believe that God is preparing me for another level of service in His church. It is for this reason that I appeal and solicit your kind and prayerful support in this campaign.

Faith is our wonderful link with our Saviour, the one who sustains us anchors the soul especially when the billows of life roll over us. Our faith is a down payment on the future and we're trusting God's invisible future.

I thank you for your support, trust and confidence. I look forward to share with you my dreams and aspiration for the Office of Bishop in our Church.

Your support is highly appreciated.

It is my prayer that the Lord will bless your ministry abundantly.

Thank you

Yours in His Service,

Andrew B. G. Lewin.

CONTACT: NAMIBIA
Rev. Willem Simon Hanse
Katutura
Namibia
Tel: +264 81 247 3022
hansew@hotmail.com

CONTACT: R.S.A
Rev. Nigel Titus
P.O. Box 10194
Caledon Square 7905
Tel. (021) 692 1550(h)
Mobile: 082 896 0208

CANDIDATE:
Rev. Andrew B.G. Lewin
P O Box 186
Plumstead 7800
Cape Town, R.S.A.
Tel: 011.2721.593 2832
Mobile: 083 382 0244
abraal@yahoo.com

Southern Africa
Tour
July 11 - 27, 2005
Johannesburg
Soweto
Kruger National Park
Swaziland
Cape Town
Zimbabwe

Tuesday, July 12, 2005

Highway sign to Sandton, Pretoria

Traveling from Johannesburg airport to the hotel in Sandton after a17-hour flight from Washington Dulles with a one-hour stop in Accra, Ghana.

Crown Plaza Hotel
Sandton, South Africa

Sandton is becoming the upscale area in South Africa, replacing Johannesburg as the banking and business hub of the country.

Rear grounds of Crown Plaza Hotel

Tuesday, July 12 - Pretoria Tour

Photo is from Barbara. Do not know the site because I opted to go to bed instead of doing a city tour which was scheduled for 2:00 p.m. We arrived in J'Burg (as the locals call it) around 11:00 a.m.

Wednesday, July 13 - Soweto Tour

Our guide in Soweto, the largest black Township in South Africa and the focal point for resistance to apartheid in the 1970's and 1980's.

Regina Mundi Church

This Catholic church has been the site of many mass gatherings over the years.

It is one of the largest churches in Africa. Bishop Desmond Tutu often addressed the people here.

One of only two Black Madonnas in South Africa can be found inside Regina Mundi church.

Seven photos

The guide is pointing to bullet holes to the church ceiling, floor, and a statue made by police who entered and shot up the church where peaceful protesters had gathered.

Thursday, July 14 - Blyde River Canyon

Left Johannesburg at 8:00 a.m. via Panorama Route to Kruger National Park.

Blyde River Canyon, the fourth largest canyon in the world. The Grand Canyon, one of the seven natural wonders of the world, is the largest.

Three photos

Kolkgate Potholes (described as Bourke's Luck Potholes in the travel info) – 5 Photos

We walked for 45-minutes to the confluence of two rivers taking in spectacular views of waterfalls, and hopping over rocks and small boulders.

On the road all day, arrived at Kruger at dusk.

Friday, July 15 - Kruger National Park

4:00 a.m. wake up. Before sunrise, collected breakfast packs, met game ranger and began game viewing in open 4x4 safari vehicles.
We were freezing! The morning and evening Temperatures were in the 40's. From 11:00am -5:00pm, the weather was beautiful -- bright, sunny, in the mid-70's.

From the open safari vehicle, the sun peaks through the trees.

We were on the hunt for the Big 5 – the Lion, Elephant, Buffalo, Leopard and Rhino.

Our first sighting -- a giraffe! The ranger drove around so that we could get a better view.

Impalas. We saw lots and lots of them.

A man made lake in Kruger Park.

The expanse of Kruger Park, which is about the size of Massachusetts. There are 155 species of mammals and 400 species of birds in the park.

This Page

Outside Kruger gift shop.

After dinner, we gathered around the fireplace for a sip of Amarula, a South African Cream Liqueur, that is made from fresh cream and fruit from the Marula tree. Cheryl, a member of our group, shared the Amarula with us.

Carolyn, Julia, Claudia, Beryl

Two more photos from Amarula gathering --

Dorothy, Pat, Connie

Two couples joined us around the fireplace to chat.

This page

Saturday, July 16 – Enroute to Swaziland

On the road to Swaziland -- a beautiful, scenic, drive with magnificent views of mountains.

Claudia and Julia on a rest/bank stop.

Carolyn, Julia, Claudia having a meal somewhere.

Sunday, July 24
Top: Leaving Zimbabwe one day late due to South African Airways' strike.

****

The following photos were taken on Wednesday, July 20, our free day in Cape Town.

Rev. Lewin showed us points of interest in Cape Town that we otherwise would not have seen.

Funeral Home - 6 photos

Who had the bright idea to visit a funeral home while on holiday? ***Julia***

Rev. Lewin, Julia, Tony Wyllie

Rev. Lewin, Claudia, Wyllie, Julia

SOUTH AFRICA
PHOTO
Printed by Fotofast
V&A Waterfront
Cape town

JERUSALEM

EGYPT

COSTA RICA

THE CARIBBEAN

Explorer of the Seas
July 28th 2001 – August 4th 2001

Welcome Aboard
INAUGURAL SEASON
Explorer of the Seas
CARIBBEAN 2001
00157482

THE BEIJING JOURNEY

03.22.2007

AUSTRAILIA &
NEWZELAND

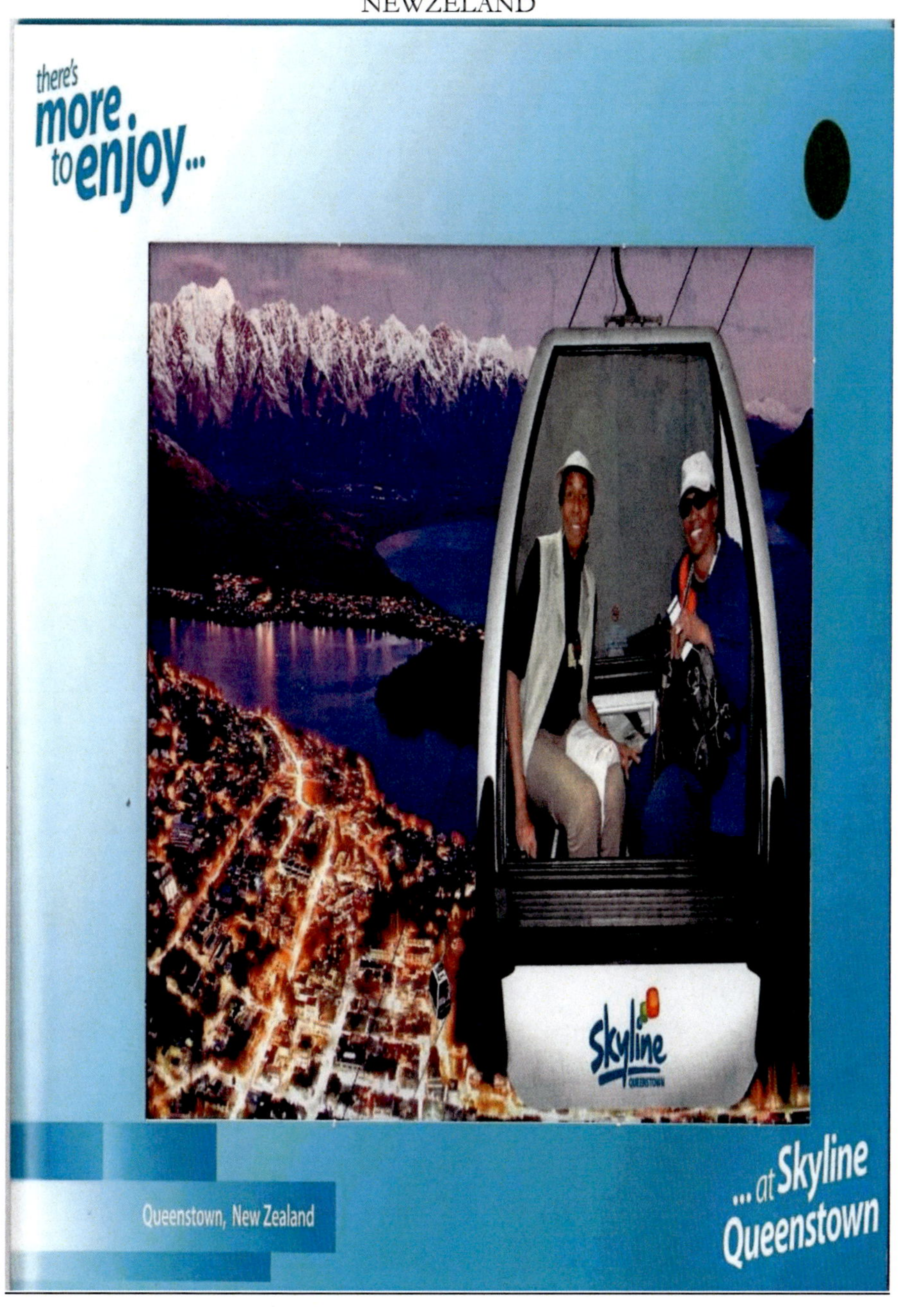

My Milford Sound
Experience

THE JOURNEY

Over the years, I have had an opportunity to travel to many amazing places such as Australia, New Zealand, China, Costa Rica, South Africa, Jamaica, the Dominican Republic, the state of Alaska, and many other places. The highlights above in picture format are some of my favorite memories from my traveling journey. While in Jerusalem, I visited David's mountaintop. King David was a mighty worshiper and warrior for God. There is no greater experience than being in the presence of God, and I pray that you will get to know Him and the power in His resurrection.

There was such a rich biblical-based historical heritage in the Holy City; I felt connected to the roots of my Christian faith and felt blessed to experience the land where many great clouds of witnesses once dwelled.

When I reflect on my experience in Egypt, I am often reminded of the historical exile in the Book of Exodus, where the mighty hand of the Lord gave the children of Israel their liberation from their enslavement. The power of God is displayed in Exodus 15:4 which states: "Pharaoh's chariots and his army he has hurled into the sea. The best of Pharaoh's officers are drowned in the Red Sea."

The mere fact that the Lord permitted the best of Pharaoh's officers to drown in the Red Sea shows that God is compassionate about the preservation of his people, his heritage, and caused the earth to back his people when the Pharaoh who was given charge over them wouldn't.

God's word is faithful to remain true as this same biblical promise to you today remains in Revelations 12:15-16: "So the serpent spewed water out of his mouth like a flood after the woman that he might cause her to be carried away by the flood. But the earth helped the woman, and the earth opened its mouth and swallowed up the flood which the dragon had spewed out of its mouth."

Therefore, if you find yourself in a position where you feel overwhelmed by barriers or challenges that you need God's help to overcome, remember that He will back you if you petition his help with prayer and have faith to believe in God for His response. Be willing to accept a yes or a no and remember that God's no is an indication that He has something better in store for you.

Speaking further on exiles, we as African Americans have our own testimony about exiles and liberation, but I want you to be mindful of the fact that many historical barriers that we've overcome must be maintained in a time where many injustices are running rampant.

The Lord is still committed to delivering the righteous from every affliction, and the Bible scripture above properly shows that the Lord is committed to and faithful in protecting His people from opposition and injustice and will continue to establish us with the power to break barriers through faith.

I am often reminded that moving forward in obedience to the voice of God is what kept the people of Israel focused on the promise. When you have losses of loved ones, riches, possessions, and friendships, remember the faithfulness of God and His willingness to call us friend. You are never alone: God will always be your help when you keep your eyes on the hill from whence cometh your help. Your help comes from the Lord!

I will conclude this book with a writing from my late-sister Eula Stokes, who, while on a trip to Alcorn College, wrote a meaningful short story, highlighting the significance of farming and agriculture in dedication to the Parker family heritage.

"A Trip to Alcorn College: The Love of Agriculture"

The man is plowing in the field. His home in the distance, his noble span of horses with all their surroundings of nature and art form a most noble picture of civilization. He is breaking the soil, the fallow ground from which springs the support of the world and without which the wheels of commerce would stop and mankind perish. Take that man and his plow from the soil and erelong, there would be no man left. I am proud of the man with the plow. He represents every element of human substance and progress, and I scorn the wretch that looks down upon him or does not appreciate him. I shall forever be thankful that I learned to labor on the farm, how to live in the sweat of an honest neighbor. – Eula L. Stokes

96435221R00104

Made in the USA
Lexington, KY
21 August 2018